Withdrawn Stock
Dorset Libraries

CLASSICAL
AUDITION
SPEECHES
for Men

In memory of
Thomas Dogget

'Who it is said took lodgings in Wapping'
in order to perfect his 'Sailor' part in
Love for Love
(performed in 1695)

CLASSICAL AUDITION SPEECHES
for Men

Jean Marlow

A&C Black · London
Heinemann · New Hampshire

First published 1996 by
A & C Black (Publishers) Limited
35 Bedford Row, London WC1R 4JH

ISBN 0–7136–4248–3

Published simultaneously in the USA by Heinemann
A Division of Reed Publishing (USA) Inc.
361 Hanover Street, Portsmouth, NH 03801–3912
Offices and Agents throughout the world

Distributed in Canada by Reed Books Canada
75 Clegg Road, Markham, Ontario L6G 1A1

ISBN 0-435-07026-6

CIP catalogue records for this book are available
from the British Library and the Library of Congress.

Typeset in 9½ on 12 pt Palatino by
Florencetype Limited, Stoodleigh, Devon

Printed in Great Britain by Redwood Books, Trowbridge, Wilts

Jean Marlow

Jean Marlow, L.G.S.M., a qualified speech and drama teacher (Guildhall School of Music and Drama), is also an actress with many years' experience in theatre, films and television.

From her early days when she worked with a group of actors, writers and directors at the Royal Court Theatre and came under the influence of George Devine, she has played roles as diverse as 'Mrs Ebury' in Tom Stoppard's *Dirty Linen* in the West End, 'Elizabeth Sawyer' in *The Witch of Edmonton*, 'Dol Common' in *Playhouse Creatures* and 'Mrs Jiniwin' in the Walt Disney classic miniseries, *The Old Curiosity Shop*. She is preparing to take part in a workshop production of Thomas Middleton's *The Witch* – one of the plays she is using in her selections from the New Mermaid series and is currently playing 'Lady Catherine de Bourgh' in the stage adaptation of *Pride and Prejudice*.

She is also Co-Director of the Actors' Theatre School and is the author of two books on auditioning and audition technique – *Actors' Audition Speeches for all ages and accents* and *Actresses' Audition Speeches for all ages and accents*. It is her untiring search for suitable audition material for our students, which has inspired this useful collection of classical speeches.

Eamonn Jones
Founder Director
The Actors' Theatre School

CONTENTS

Classical Audition Speeches

Preface

Finding suitable audition speeches is an on-going problem for both students and professional actors alike – particularly when looking for good classical material which has not been over-used. Most students preparing an audition speech for drama school read the word 'classical' in the audition requirements and look no further than Shakespeare. This is an easy option. Local bookshops and libraries usually have a 'Complete Works of Shakespeare', whereas other classical plays are more difficult, or even impossible, to track down at short notice. This is a great pity because, although Shakespeare is undoubtedly our greatest playwright, there is an enormous wealth and variety of other classical work being sadly neglected. Auditioners get tired of listening to the same old pieces being trotted out again and again, and the Royal Academy of Dramatic Art in London have even gone as far as to publish a list of those speeches they simply don't want to hear any more!

In these two books of *Classical Audition Speeches* – one for men and one for women – I have endeavoured to include selections that are not so well known, and perhaps some that may never have been used until now. There are some splendid dramatic opportunities in *The Revenger's Tragedy*, *'Tis Pity She's a Whore*, and *The Duchess of Malfi*, as well as some very funny speeches such as one by 'Hardcastle' in *She Stoops to Conquer* teaching his stupid servants to wait at table. You will also find a variety of accents, for example 'Timothy Tapwell' from *A New Way to Pay Old Debts* with his strong Nottinghamshire dialect, among many others. All the selections have been taken from the New Mermaid series of classical plays, and can be found in most bookshops and bigger libraries. Each has an introduction which is very readable and is packed with really useful background information for actors.

All the speeches have been tried and tested by students at the Actors' Theatre School, either in class or in auditions or outside drama examinations – so they really do work!

I hope these books will not only fulfil a need for students and professional actors looking for fresh material, but also provide a quick and handy reference when the telephone rings with that unexpected audition for one of the lesser-known classical plays.

Acknowledgements

I would like to say thank you to the actors, directors, play-wrights, casting directors, agents and organisations who have helped me with this book, including:

Michael Attenborough, Nicholas Barter, Richard Carpenter, Frances Cuka, George Cuttingham, Gillian Diamond, Patrick Duggan, Margaret Hamilton, Rona Laurie, Peter Layton, Jacky Leggo, Malcolm Morrison, Sue Parrish, Paul Peters, Brian Schwartz, of Offstage Bookshop in London, Keith Salberg, Don Taylor, Di Trevis, Mervyn Wycherley, Amieth Yogarajah.

And not forgetting my co-director, Eamonn Jones, without whom this book would never have been compiled, and the students themselves who tried out all these audition speeches for me.

Introduction

When I was at school we were forced to study Shakespeare, Ben Jonson and Christopher Marlowe. I hated them all. I was sent to elocution classes because I spoke badly. The teacher was a great believer in Shakespeare as a cure for a London accent, and there I was, at the age of twelve, being 'Cleopatra' bitten by an asp, writhing all over her front room carpet, and a most unlikely 'Julius Caesar'. Then came the end of term play, and because they knew I was taking elocution classes, I was chosen to play 'Oberon' in *A Midsummer Night's Dream*. I was squeezed into a tight green silk costume that just about covered my podgy figure, and I had to sing:

> I know a bank whereon the wild thyme blows
> Where oxlips and the nodding violet grows . . .

The tune still haunts me. I have a vivid memory of tripping over the uneven green canvas that had been used to cover the school swimming pool as I made my hurried exit, looking more like Toad of Toad Hall than the King of the Fairies.

Scenes like this stick in your mind and it took three years of drama school to overcome an uneasy feeling when anyone mentioned 'the classics'. Some people never recover. I remember one of my first jobs in the theatre where the leading lady had it written into her contract, that whenever the company put on a classical play she had a 'fortnight out'.

This was a long time ago, but the same feeling often prevails today. A sixteen year old student told me he had never studied any Shakespeare. The class had 'voted him out', he said. (Perhaps their parents had had similar experiences to mine.) 'What about the other classics?' I asked. He didn't know. Anyway, they were going to do a modern play instead!

So let's try and clear up a few misconceptions concerning 'the classics'. The word 'classic' according to Webster's Dictionary means 'a work of enduring excellence'. Therefore all the speeches in this book are taken from plays of 'enduring excellence'. They 'endured' because they entertained and enlightened audiences for many years and continue to do so today. They are the very

1

best of their kind and we should be grateful for the opportunity to play them, not see them as some sort of stumbling block.

Recently, a ten year old student of mine went to see a performance of *Dr Faustus* at his big brother's school. 'They had a candle on stage, burning all the way through. That represented Faustus' life,' he said. 'At the end of the play when the devils got him, the candle was blown out and the stage was all dark. It was good. I liked it.' So that school, at least, saw Christopher Marlowe's play as an entertainment, not an academic exercise.

The days of performing 'the classics' in a declamatory style with exaggerated gestures, a pained expression and the 'voice beautiful' are thankfully over. Directors nowadays have very different, and often controversial, ideas on how Shakespeare, Marlowe and Jonson should be played. Barry Rutter, Artistic Director of the Northern Broadsides Company, uses northern actors, thereby celebrating 'the spontaneity, unpredictability and festivity of theatre using classic texts with a coherent voice style firmly rooted in the North of England'. However, I agree with Rona Laurie, who in her recent book, *The Actor's Art and Craft*, said: 'It is important for an actor who wishes to play a range of parts, including classical ones, to have, in addition to any regional accent he may speak, a pure enunciation of vowel sounds . . . '

Many students and professional actors shy away from the classics, imagining that you have to have some sort of academic background in order to play them. In fact it is often better to start from nothing – with no preconceived ideas. The characters in Ben Jonson's *The Alchemist* are 'low life' Londoners. They fight, they lie, they cheat and they steal, and you don't have to be an academic with a 'posh' accent to do that. But you do need, as Barrie Rutter says, 'a coherent voice style'. Your voice has to carry and you have to be heard at the back of the auditorium.

But let's take a look at the first audition most of us encounter when we consider 'going into the theatre' or joining 'the rogues and vagabonds' as the Elizabethans might term it – the drama school audition.

Applying and Auditioning for Drama School

You want to become an actor and you've decided, quite rightly in most cases, that the best way to go about it is to apply for Drama School. Twenty or thirty years ago you might have been able to 'get a start' in one of the smaller theatre companies as an 'ASM playing small parts', that is an Assistant Stage Manager, prompting, helping out backstage generally, playing the odd parts of maid, butler or policeman as they came up, and hopefully learning your job that way. But today, with fewer theatres available and most of those unwilling, or unable to take on extra staff, it is unlikely that you'd even be considered. And writing to fringe theatre trying to get the odd line or two, or working as an extra in films and television, is not going to do you much good. Of course there are young people who are 'discovered' and never went to drama school or had an acting lesson in their lives. They were lucky, if you can call it that. And you can't run your life on luck. The theatre is a precarious business and you've got to give yourself the best possible chance in order to succeed.

Now you've contacted the various schools and asked them to send you a prospectus and application form. The prospectus should outline the courses offered and explain what will be required of you at your audition. Drama courses in Great Britain can be very expensive and it is best to make absolutely sure you can afford the school of your choice before sending off your form and audition fee. Not all local councils, or in the case of students from overseas, governments, are prepared to assist these days. One student was told by his council that they could train five engineers with the money it takes to send a single actor to drama school. Never mind – a few drama schools are now offering degree courses (BA Drama), and councils are inclined to look more favourably on these. You will also find some universities offering drama courses, but these tend to be more academic.

In the United States there are very few vocational drama schools such as the Royal Academy of Dramatic Art (RADA) or the Guildhall School of Music and Drama in London. The equivalent would be the American Academy of Dramatic Arts or the Juilliard School in New York. Most drama courses are affiliated to universities, such as Yale, and are again very expensive. There are no grants available, but you may qualify for a student loan. If you elect to go to drama school there are scholarships you can apply for, or you could approach one of the various Foundations (i.e. organisations or trusts), such as The Carnegie-Mellon Foundation, for a theatre bursary or scholarship. When you have selected the school that has the most to offer you and have sent in your fee and application form, do make sure you have read the audition requirements thoroughly. You really should apply for more than one school as you rarely get accepted on a first audition, although it has been known. Classical speeches in particular get better the more they are performed and there is no doubt about it, you develop a way of handling auditions. At your second attempt you will not be nearly so nervous and you will begin to look around you and compare notes with others who are experiencing the same thing as yourself. Your first couple of auditions should, I think, be treated as a learning process.

Most schools require you to perform two contrasting speeches of about three minutes each, one modern and one classical, often stipulating that the classical speech must be in verse. Sometimes you are asked to prepare a song and given some movement and improvisation to do. A few schools ask for three prepared speeches, although they may not even ask to hear the third, and others send out a list of about ten selections, ask you to pick out one or sometimes two of them, and then contrast these with a piece of your own choice. All speeches and the song must be learnt by heart. It is surprising how many would-be drama students think all they have to do is to just stand up and read everything!

Choosing a suitable audition piece

Whether you are choosing a classical or modern speech, it is best to find a part that is near to your own age and experience, unless of course you have a particular talent or liking for playing older or younger parts convincingly.

4

Do make sure that you read the audition requirements *carefully*, particularly with regard to your classical speech. Sometimes you may be given two or even three periods to choose from. There is no point picking out a speech from a Restoration comedy that you rather like if they have asked for something from an Elizabethan or Jacobean drama, written in blank verse.

The speeches in this book are mainly from plays written in the following periods:

Elizabethan (1558–1603)
Including among others, speeches from the tragedies, *Arden of Faversham*, *Edward the Second* and the comedy *The Shoemaker's Holiday*. All selections are in verse.

Jacobean (1603–1625)
Including selections from *The Duchess of Malfi*, *The Revenger's Tragedy*, *Bartholmew Fair* and *Eastward Ho!*. Again the majority of these are written in verse, with the exception of the last two comedies mentioned, which are in prose.

Restoration (1660–1710)
This is the period following Charles II's return from France – the Restoration of the Monarchy – and for the first time in England actresses appeared on stage. The speeches included are mostly taken from Restoration comedies such as *The Way of the World* and *The Relapse* and are written in prose, the notable exception being Dryden's tragedy, *All for Love* which is written in blank verse.

Late Eighteenth Century
Including speeches from such comedies as *The Rivals* and *The School for Scandal* – all written in prose.

Late Nineteenth Century
Including speeches from the comedies of Oscar Wilde, such as *The Importance of Being Earnest* and *Lady Windermere's Fan*. All written in prose.

Contrast

Contrast is an important word in the theatre. Contrast keeps an audience from becoming bored – and an auditioner too. Look at those audition requirements and you will see the word 'contrast'. Contrast your speeches. If you have already selected something dramatic, contrast it with a comedy, or try something with a different accent. Shakespeare is, as I have already said, our greatest playwright, but it is good to ring the changes sometimes and look further afield. In America they lay less emphasis on Shakespeare and encourage students to look at work by some of his contemporaries as well.

The Drama Centre London, one of the schools that send out a list of classical speeches to choose from, included selections from John Ford's *'Tis Pity She's a Whore* last season. A German student of mine gained a place at Drama Centre with 'Giovanni's' opening speech from *'Tis Pity She's a Whore*, contrasting it with a modern piece from a Neil Simon play. And an Italian student used 'Hippolita's' speech from the same Ford play, contrasting it with a speech from a Dario Fo play and won a place at the E15 Acting School. Both classical speeches are included in these books.

Preparation

If you look at the front of this book you will see that I have dedicated it to Thomas Dogget (1670–1721) – a fine actor and famous as a 'low comedian'. It is said that at the age of twenty–five he took lodgings in Wapping in order to prepare himself for his role as the sailor 'Ben', in *Love for Love* – a part written especially for him by the playwright William Congreve. Other actors in this comedy, which opened at the new playhouse in Lincoln's Inn Fields, London, included Thomas Betterton and the great Elizabeth Barry, but it was Dogget who was considered to be the greatest success of the production. How many young or, for that matter, older actors would go to that much trouble to perfect a part? He was extremely popular as an all-round entertainer – he could also sing – and was perhaps a Max Wall or Jimmy Jewell of his time. Thirteen years later he played the foolish old knight, 'Sir Paul Plyant', in Congreve's *The Double-Dealer* and was mentioned for his 'Unparrell'd' performance.

Read the Play

The very first step in your preparation is to read the play. I cannot overemphasise the importance of this. You owe it to the playwright and you owe it to yourself. Many students simply cannot see the point of this, particularly as they are only preparing one speech, not performing the whole play. The point is that you need to know whom you are talking to in this particular speech. 'Does it matter?' one student said to me. Of course it matters. It matters very much indeed. Your attitude to the character or characters you are speaking to alters according to the sort of people they are, their motives and your motives for speaking to them. Are they friends or enemies? People you love, people you hate, or people you are indifferent to? What has happened in the previous scene? What has just been said that makes you react in a particular way? Is your speech in answer to a question? If you don't know the question, how can you possibly answer?

'Balthazar's' speech from *The Spanish Tragedy* begins:

Both well, and ill: it makes me glad and sad . . .

This is obviously in reply to a question. But what is that question and who has asked it? It is vital to the speech to know both these things. I have given you the answers in the introduction to this speech. But you need to know a good deal more about the build up to this scene, and the relationship between the characters at this point in time.

You need to read and reread the play. Gather as much information as you can about your character and ask yourself:

1. What does your character say or think about himself?
2. What does he say or think about the other characters in the play?
3. What do they say about him?
4. What has happened in the previous scene?
5. What does your character want?
   a) In this particular scene?
   b) Throughout the play?
6. What is the playwright's intention in this scene? Are we meant to laugh or cry?
7. Each character is making a journey. At what stage in the journey are you when you are performing this speech?

7

Sometimes, of course, the information given in the play is insufficient and you need to look further.

'Jack Pinchwife' in *The Country Wife* has discovered his wife writing yet another affectionate letter to 'Mister Horner'. At the end of his speech he raises his sword as if to kill her. What did it mean to a man to be made 'a cuckold' in those days?

Try to find out as much as you can about the period the play is written in and what was the social and political situation at that time, or in that country?

All the above information is essential to the process of building up your character.

Language

Classical plays tend to be written in heightened language and often, as in the case of the Elizabethan and Jacobean period, in blank verse. And so we need to learn and practise additional skills in order to perform them so that an audience can both hear and understand us.

Blank verse means verse that does not rhyme, but has a recognisable rhythm – and fortunately the rhythm used by most playwrights in this period is the one we use now in everyday speech. It is the measure, pulse or pattern most natural to the English language; an unstressed syllable followed by a stressed syllable. When actors understand this, they find speaking in blank verse very much easier than they thought, and realise they don't need to declaim it in tortured tones or stand up and recite it like a poem. The speeches in this collection come from plays, and plays are meant to be acted not 'speechified'.

You will hear people talk of the metre of verse and I think it's important for actors to know at least something about this. Metre is simply the 'grammar of rhythm' or, in other words, how the rhythm is technically described. Blank verse is usually written in 'five foot iambic metre'. Such a line consists of five 'feet'. Each *iambic* foot is a pair of syllables where the first syllable is unstressed, the second stressed. Each iambic foot is written like this: ⌣—. And so a regular line of blank verse can be written:

⌣—/⌣—/⌣—/⌣—/⌣—

We would write down a single line of verse from 'Flamineo's' speech from *The White Devil* like this:

8

This night / I'll know / the ut / most of / my fate

⏑ — / ⏑ — / ⏑ — / ⏑ — / ⏑ —

However, if we followed this metre exactly it would sound like a child reciting:

de dum / de dum / de dum / de dum / de dum

So now we have to place the stresses so that the line makes sense, while not disrupting the structure of the verse. An actor playing 'Flamineo' might well put a heavy stress on the whole of the word 'utmost', but certainly would not put the same stress on the word 'of'. This is, of course, a matter for individual choice.

Not every line of blank verse is regular and it is the irregularities that give interest and very often a clue to how the playwright intended the line to be said. Very often you find a heavy stress at the beginning of a line, sometimes an extra unstressed syllable at the end, occasionally a line that is very short indeed.

There are many instances in blank verse where there is no punctuation at the end of a line and you need to read straight on to the next line until it makes sense, as for example 'Faustus's' speech from *Dr Faustus*:

Had I as many souls as there be stars
I'd give them all for Mephastophilis

It is usual for the voice to rise/or inflect upwards where the sentence or thought is incomplete, and downwards when the thought or sentence is completed. You do this in modern English. The sense here runs on from the first line and over into the second. And so you need to have an upward inflection at the end of the first line to indicate that the sense runs on, and also a very slight pause to show that it is the end of a verse line – again we have to be careful not to spoil the structure of the verse.

Most people agree that you should not take a breath at the end of a line where the sense runs on, but there are of course exceptions to this rule, depending sometimes on a particular characterisation or mood, and often on the director's own ideas on the subject!

When another character's line or lines have been deleted in a speech written in verse, as in Giovanni's speech in *'Tis Pity She's a Whore*, I have indicated where the Friar's line ('Yes, you may love, fair son.') is cut, as follows:

> ... Must I not praise
> That beauty which, if framed anew, the gods
> Would make a god of, if they had it there, ... etc.

The first part of the verse line is obviously missing and you need to be aware of this and compensate with a pause, or perhaps a move towards or away from the Friar.

Not all Elizabethan and Jacobean speeches are written in verse. The speeches from *Bartholmew Fair* are all in prose and even in most of the verse plays, the comedians and 'low life' characters usually speak prose. 'Almachildes's' speech from *The Witch* is written in both verse and prose.

As we move into the Restoration period (1660–1710), the popular comedies of the day were written in prose, but their exuberant and often flamboyant style needs considerable vocal technique, as do the plays of the late eighteenth and nineteenth centuries. Long lines and extended images demand good breath control at the very least.

Words

Very often if you speak words you are unfamiliar with it can get in the way of your performance. You feel unnatural saying them and it shows. Another good reason for reading the play! Most editions, certainly the New Mermaid series of classical plays, give meanings of words and expressions that you wouldn't normally find in your dictionary, and you need to keep practising these until they roll easily off your tongue. 'Ben' in *Love for Love* uses many sea-faring expressions in the scene where he woos 'Miss Prue' and although it is a very funny speech, you need to work hard to get the humour out of it. Expressions like 'mayhap I may steer into your harbour' and words such as 'gad' and 'forsooth', all need a lot of practice until they become familiar. Improvisation can be of great help here, and it is often useful to try putting difficult speeches into your own words.

Voice and Speech

Many people imagine that voice and speech are one and the same thing. They are not. Voice is the sound we make and speech is the way in which we shape that sound in order to communicate with others. Whether performing in a modern or a classical play the most important thing for an actor is to be clearly heard. I remember seeing a final year production at one of the bigger drama schools and I found one of the players extremely difficult to hear. When I commented on this afterwards, I was told it didn't matter because 'she'd be doing television'. Even on television you need a certain degree of clarity and the sound man often has to tell an actor to 'speak up!' or give him 'a bit more voice'.

Obviously classical speeches put extra demands on the voice. You need good vocal control to manage two, and sometimes three, lines of verse in one breath, or convey extended images of thought without chopping up or losing the sense. Ends of words also need to be considered – 't' or 'd' must not be missed off – and 'street cred' is definitely out.

A voice needs to be taken care of and exercised daily. No ballet dancer would dream of going on stage without some sort of 'warm-up' or exercise, so why should it be any different for an actor? There is not enough space here to outline voice and speech routines, but I would advise you to work on a few simple breathing exercises each day, together with perhaps a few 'tongue twisters' to firm up the beginnings and ends of your words. Malcolm Morrison in his excellent book, *Classical Acting*, gives some good basic exercises, but he also comments that although there are many good books on voice and speech, 'these do not replace work done with a good teacher'.

Movement

It is important to move well and with confidence on stage, but it is also important to consider the period your character is from. Movement is affected by costume. For example, what sort of shoes is your character wearing? These will certainly affect your walk. The heavily padded sleeves of the Elizabethan gentleman will ensure that gestures are wide – no modern jerky movements, and the head will be held erect according to the amount of starching and depth of ruff at the neck. Have a look at costume books and perhaps the paintings of the Restoration period. Hats were wide-brimmed and trimmed with feathers and were carried when not being worn. Men wore wigs; these were later to become huge and ridiculous, restricting head turns. They wore lace collars and long lace cuffs, making a difference to the way they raised a glass of wine to their lips. They wore petticoat breeches, again with lots of lace and ribbon. The calf of the leg was considered a great attribute; they wore high cuban heels and braced their legs to accentuate this.

It is interesting to note that even in 1592 actors were warned against unnecessary movements '. . . And this I bar, over and besides, that none of you stroke your beards to make action, play with your cod-piece points, or stand fumbling on your buttons when you know not how to bestow your fingers'. Thomas Nashe. I wonder what advice he would have given to actresses, had there been any around in those days!

Of course Thomas Nashe was referring to fidgeting on stage, and often today you see students standing like sticks, arms straight at their sides, clenching and unclenching their hands while they deliver their speech. There is also the temptation among the more confident, to overdo movement and gesture, waving the arms about in a supposedly Elizabethan, Restoration or Victorian manner. Let's face it, we're talking about a three minute audition speech. If you used the proportionate amount of gesture throughout the whole play, you'd be flailing about like a windmill all evening. Every movement and gesture should be properly motivated. A good motto might be, 'When in doubt leave it out'.

What do I wear at the audition?

Most schools tell you what to wear at your audition, particularly if they are starting with some sort of warm-up or movement session. The main thing is to be comfortable. If you know there is going to be movement and improvisation, wear something casual – tights, trousers and jazz shoes (the ones with small heels) are easy to work in. You have to bear in mind your classical speech, and blue jeans and trainers can look a bit silly if you are playing a very formal character. It can sometimes be helpful to take a jacket or waistcoat along with you. I think

12

dressing in black looks good at this sort of audition, and you can always add on, or take off 'extra bits' for your second or third speech.

If the speech is too long

The majority of speeches in this book are between three and four minutes in length – an acceptable time for most auditions. However, there are occasions when you are specifically required to limit your time to two or even one and a half minutes. If you go over this time you are liable to be stopped before you get to the end, and if you rush it you will spoil your performance. Be bold – cut it down to the required length. This is not nearly as difficult as it might seem. For instance 'Ferdinand's' speech from *The Duchess of Malfi* can be cut considerably by finishing on:

> And for my sake thou hast done much ill will.

And 'Tony Lumpkin's' speech from *She Stoops to Conquer* finishes neatly on:

> ... I fairly lodged them in the horse pond at the
> bottom of the garden.

If a speech cannot be reduced easily, or you feel by cutting it you will lose sense or quality, have a look through the play. The character may well have another speech lasting only a minute and a half.

Should you have coaching?

A lot of drama schools say they don't want to see a carefully drilled performance and I agree with them. However, I do think you need some help and advice from a trusted, experienced actor or teacher. A few tips on 'voice' and the 'speaking of blank verse' certainly wouldn't go amiss. For instance, a student came to see me, having carefully re-typed her classical audition speech from blank verse into prose. She proudly handed me half a dozen copies saying, 'These should be useful for you and so much easier to read'.

I hope what I have said in these pages has been helpful and not too daunting. As you can see, classical speeches need a lot of extra work. But if in doubt – concentrate on the acting. Remember a drama school is looking for potential, not perfection.

George Cuttingham

I asked George Cuttingham, President of the American Academy of Dramatic Arts, in New York, to give a few words of advice to students performing classical speeches for the first time:

> At the American Academy of Dramatic Arts, we see classical material as presenting the actor with a dual challenge: to speak lines that are often far removed from everyday conversation (lines that are often rich with wit and poetic imagery and seething with exalted emotion), and to do so with the same quality of honest, personal connection – to the dramatic circumstance, to one's own feelings and to other actors – that is desirable when acting simple contemporary material.
>
> While untrained actors will not usually have the vocal development and verbal skills to do full justice to classical material, they can still audition effectively if they speak the lines clearly and simply, without indicating emotion they do not feel, remembering that the character is a human being with something to say and a reason for saying it, not someone intent on demonstrating perfect vowel sounds.

Nicholas Barter

Nicholas Barter, Principal of the Royal Academy of Dramatic Art in London, had this to say:

> The Royal Academy of Dramatic Art (RADA) auditions between 1400 and 1500 students a year for 30 available places.
>
> Applicants are required to present a contrasting classical speech and a modern speech. With so many auditioning it is always advisable to avoid speeches which the audition panel sees over and over again. Try to find a classical piece that suits your age and temperament. Make sure you read the whole play so that you know the context of the scene and be prepared to look outside the better known Shakespeare speeches when preparing something from the sixteenth or seventeenth centuries. Learn the speech thoroughly, making sure you understand the meaning of every word and the kind of character you are playing. Above all, make it real and truthful.

Rona Laurie

And finally, Rona Laurie, ex-actress, well-known drama coach and experienced auditioner, has this to say about the importance of choosing good material:

Both the winner and runner-up in this year's Drama Student of the Year Competition sponsored by *The Stage* and *Theatre World* chose classical speeches to perform in the final. Very few of the twenty-six actors competing in the preceding round at Wembley Exhibition Centre had gone to Elizabethan and Jacobean plays for their choice. As one of the panel of three judges I had no doubt in my mind of the advantage that their choice of classical speeches had given the two successful students. There were, I believe three main reasons.

First, of course, the quality and power of the language, secondly the dramatic impact of the playwrights' creation of situation and, thirdly, the fact that the speeches came so freshly to the ears of a panel long-accustomed to a repetitive repertoire of over-used audition speeches from modern plays, and not always the best plays available.

My advice to anyone looking for audition material would be to search for the best plays of their kind. Several of the performers we saw obviously had promise but failed to rise above the poor quality of their speeches.

In the field of classical drama, particularly in the Elizabethan and Jacobean periods there is still a wealth of exciting, comparatively unused material to be found.

Auditioning for Professional Theatre

After completing drama school you will continue to audition in some form or other throughout your career, even if it is only an 'interview' with perhaps an invitation to 'come in and read the script'. However, if you have had: some solid stage training; have worked on your voice and movement; have had the opportunity of developing various characters and learning to play opposite other actors without 'falling over the furniture', you stand a better chance of gaining professional employment and staying in the 'business'. Even from a practical point of view, at the end of your drama school training you will be performing in front of agents and casting directors in your final productions, and you will stand a chance of being selected for representation or be given the opportunity of auditioning for a professional theatre company. For those who are thinking in terms of films and television only, I would mention that you usually come by this sort of work because someone has seen you performing on stage in the first place. Very few film and television directors are going to take a risk on casting a young actor or actress with no professional experience whatsoever, and the best way to gain this experience is in the theatre.

'Getting a start' can be a major problem, but by now you should have a fairly wide range of audition speeches, gathered together over your two to three years as a student.

Your very first audition could well be for a repertory or a summer stock company (if you are in the United States), where a different play is presented every two or three weeks, sometimes monthly and in a few rare exceptions these days, weekly. I spoke to Agent and Personal Manager, Jacky Leggo who had this to say:

> Most theatre companies ask for one classical and one modern piece to be prepared when auditioning. It is very useful to be able to refer to a choice of classical speeches in one book, as very often these auditions are arranged at short notice, leaving an artiste little research time. Many people choose Shakespearean speeches when asked for something classical,

but it is important to have a varied choice, to avoid a Director hearing the same pieces over and over again.

Try to find out what plays are listed for the season, and use speeches that are appropriate, especially for your classic selection. If you know they are putting on an Oscar Wilde play there is not much point in presenting a piece from a Jacobean revenge play. If you are auditioning for a company presenting plays in repertoire, i.e. a company which performs a number of plays, rotating them regularly, then the same things applies. London, of course, capitalises on this system with the Royal National Theatre and Royal Shakespeare companies planning their programmes so that tourists and visitors can see as many as four plays within a fortnight.

Be warned! It is important to keep your audition selections 'brushed up' – or at least go over the words every now and then. As Jacky Leggo has already confirmed, many of these companies expect actors to be able to audition at a moment's notice. Recently a company auditioning for 'Phaedra' expected a piece of Greek tragedy prepared within forty eight hours, and it's not unknown for a certain well-known company to ring up actors the night before and ask them to bring a piece of verse from one of the classics to perform the following morning!

It is also a good idea to refresh your memory about language (see page 8). It's only too easy when you are called to a last minute audition, to hastily revise a piece of classical verse, forgetting that it *is* verse, ignoring the rhythm and where the breaths should come, and turn it into a piece of prose. I know, I've done it myself!

Frequently an actor or actress is asked to audition for one specific part in a particular production. It could be a tour, a play coming into the West End of London, or in the United States – a Broadway or off-Broadway production. This is an entirely different sort of audition, where suitability often counts more than capability. You are not likely to be asked to play 'Jack Pinchwife' in *The Country Wife* if you are only twenty–two, and 'Sir Lucius O'Trigger' in *The Rivals* needs a good, if not genuine, Irish accent. You will most certainly be asked to read or sight-read and will be judged on your suitability for the part, i.e. age, appearance, build, voice-range, etc.

A word about reading or sight-reading

In theatre, films, television and radio, being asked to read or sight-read for a part are one and the same thing. It means that you will be given a script to read that you have never seen before and be expected to give some sort of reasonable performance, or at least a good indication of how you would play the part. You may be given a few minutes to look through it, but sometimes you only have time for a quick glance and then have to begin reading. You should try to look up from the page as much as possible, so that the auditioner can see your face and also so that the words are 'lifted' from the page, rather than looking down all the time and mumbling into your script. Sight-reading is a skill that can be learnt and practised until you can eventually hold a line, or part of a line, in your head and look up where appropriate, instead of being hampered by having to look down all the time. If you are asked to read blank verse don't let yourself be panicked and don't be rushed into your reading. Ask if you can have a couple of minutes to look through it. Glance down the right-hand side of the verse lines and note where there is no punctuation at the end of the line and the sense runs over to the next line, so that you can make sure that you don't take a breath at that point. Take your time. If some of the words are unknown to you or difficult to pronounce, don't stop or say 'sorry', just carry on with confidence. Sometimes verse is easier to read than prose, as you'll find you can retain more of it in 'your mind's eye'.

Fringe theatre in this country, and off off-Broadway in the United States, has proliferated as many commercial and subsidised companies have had to close down. Most of these operate in pub theatres or in small arts centres. Several are experimental and of a very high standard indeed, but unfortunately not well funded, and 'profit share' has become a euphemism, with rare exceptions, for 'no money for the cast' or 'expenses only'. However, it gives actors who are not working a chance to be seen by directors and casting directors, and there is considerable competition for some of the better parts. Mostly, as in paid theatre, you will be required to read and sometimes asked to prepare a modern or classical speech. Some excellent classic plays are produced on the fringe, *Love for Love* is being performed as I write this, and it can be one of the best ways of gaining experience and adding to your C.V.

18

Advice from the actors

I spoke to two well-known actors, who have performed in some of the plays from which these speeches were taken, and asked them if they would give some tips and advice on auditioning for classic plays, and perhaps tell us a little about their own experience on these occasions.

Patrick Duggan

Irish actor, Patrick Duggan, who trained at the Dublin Gate Theatre with the Edwards MacLiammoir Company, was recently in the West End production of *Philadelphia, Here I Come*, played 'Father Murphy' in the television comedy series, *The Upper Hand* and is currently appearing in BBC Television's *EastEnders*, had this to say:

Reading for a part in a classic presents difficulties not found in doing so for a part in a modern play. The strangeness of the language and the lack of familiar terms of reference can prevent quick characterisation.

I encountered these difficulties in abundance when asked by director Stephen Unwin to read for the part of 'Foigard' in the English Touring Theatre's production of *The Beaux' Stratagem* by George Farquhar. 'Foigard' is an Irish cleric, who for reasons never made quite clear, is pretending to be Belgian. His dialogue is an almost crazed mixture of stage-Irish and stage-continental. Halfway through my reading I stopped and asked if I was on the right track.

'It's wonderful,' said Stephen.

'Don't get carried away,' I said to myself.

'"Wonderful" doesn't necessarily mean you've got the part!'

I think that one should not be afraid to ask a director such a question, nor to reread a line or passage if not satisfied with one's rendering. There is no reason for an audition to be a shot in the dark. Speak up!

For the record . . . in this case 'Wonderful' did mean I had got the part.

When I read for the part of 'Philly Cullen' in Lindsay Anderson's production of Synge's *Playboy of the Western World* I felt on very certain ground indeed.

I had played the part twice before, on radio and on the stage, so I was very familiar with Synge's heightened version of Irish speech. Also, being Irish myself the accent presented no problem. Not that accent need present a problem. Many actors and actresses are obsessed with getting an accent right. Often at the expense of believable characterisation and the suppression of personality. I believe that it is much more important to produce the cadences of an accent than to waste time trying for what, in fact, can never sound 'authentic', for the simple reason that it is not.

Lindsay Anderson was not impressed by my genuine authenticity . . . he didn't give me the part. So there!

Frances Cuka

Then I spoke to Frances Cuka, a Royal Shakespeare and Royal National Theatre player, working in this country and in the States, who made her name as 'Jo' in *A Taste of Honey* in the West End and more recently as 'Mrs Nickleby' in *Nicholas Nickleby* on Broadway, and 'Mrs Dudgeon' in the Royal National Theatre's *The Devil's Disciple*.

When I was a lot younger I went up for a part in a Restoration comedy, for one of those saucy maid's parts, knowing, witty and sexy, who usually wears a dress cut down to the nipples. I knew the director and knew he liked my work. After the audition I had a rather smart lunch date, so I had gone along wearing my best black suit and high-heeled shoes. My director friend looked stricken. 'Can you come back in a couple of days' time, wearing something more suitable?' he asked. – Two days later I returned, this time wearing a full skirt, low-necked blouse and a belt that nipped me in at the waist. I read for him and got the job.

Another director friend, considered very avant-garde in his day, once told me that when he was casting a period play he would never consider any girl who turned up wearing jeans and T-shirt. Psychologically he found it rather insulting to himself, he felt it showed arrogance, and/or sloppiness on the actress's part and made his job of ascertaining her worth more difficult. Both directors were men of imagination and fanatical attention to detail. Striking a wrong note as you walk in the door can seriously hamper your chance of getting the part.

Work on your voice, the dialogue can be deceptively simple, sometimes convoluted, but there should be a naturalness about the delivery, and good diction is essential. If you have done the very best you can, you still may not get the job, because the director didn't think you were quite suitable, but he or she may remember you for another production later.

When you do a Restoration play you go back in time, in dress and dialogue, but not in humanity. There are real people under those periwigs. They may be greedy, sex-obsessed and bitchy, so what's new? My favourite character is all of these things. 'Lady Wishfort' in *The Way of the World* is a domestic tyrant who forbids her niece to marry the man she loves, because 'Lady Wishfort' fancies him herself. Laughed at and plotted against by the younger people for being a widow of fifty–five still on the lookout for a man, 'Lady Wishfort' ploughs through the play like a great battleship, past her prime but indomitable, trailing streamers of glory. Her rages are tremendous – 'Ods my life, I'll have him. I'll have him murdered. I'll have him poisoned. Where does he eat?' – and topical – 'I warrant the spendthrift-prodigal's in debt as much as a million lottery, or the whole court upon a birthday.' After this rage has subsided, her make-up has cracked and needs repairing. 'I look like an old peeled wall.' 'Foible', her maid, busy repairing the damage observes, 'A little art once made your picture like you, and now a little of the same art must make you like your picture. Your picture must sit for you, Madam'. Aah – it comes to us all in the end. Yet her recklessness and lust for life sustain her. At the end of the play, when all the plots against her have been revealed, she accepts defeat with dignity, though I'm not so sure that she won't be on the rampage a week or so later. If you look at the cast list of *The Way of the World* there are an equal number of men and women, six parts each and that's missing out two women, 'Betty' and 'Peg', both small parts.

Restoration plays show a good ratio of women's parts, good women's parts, and for a very good reason. When the Monarchy was restored, so was the theatre – under the Parliamentarians everything that was enjoyable was a sin, and the theatres, being thoroughly sinful, were closed down. Now they were open for business again with a new novelty guaranteed to pull in the punters. Instead of boys there were real women playing the women's parts! And the public flocked to see this new phenomenon. The playwrights responded with a cornucopia of lovely ladies – randy, argumentative, bitchy, conniving, mincing (the name of a maid in *The Way of the World*), flouncing and strutting, women in breeches, even a

21

female Casanova who fought duels. So when you audition for one of these feisty beings you can't be a shy violet. Even the Goody-two-Shoes, the friend of the heroine and second love interest, is intelligent and witty and a better part than you get in most modern plays. You mustn't slouch – those ladies with their low-necked dresses and laced-in waists knew they were being looked over, and flaunted what they'd got. They arrived on stage, never to depart, and they knew their value. Try to read these plays as they read them, new and exciting and fresh, not some old play that's been around for donkey's years. The gold's still there – it's up to you to make it glitter.

What directors and casting directors look for

What are auditioners looking for when they ask you to prepare a classical speech or invite you to audition for a specific part in an Elizabethan, Jacobean, Restoration or late eighteenth- or nineteenth-century play?

Gillian Diamond

I spoke to Gillian Diamond – Head of Casting with the Royal National Theatre for fifteen years and also the Royal Shakespeare Company, and now Associate Producer for the Sir Peter Hall Company – who runs a course at the Drama Centre, preparing third year students for entry into the profession – and she had this to say:

For general auditions, read the play carefully and choose wisely to suit your character and your strengths. Try to be original. If it is a piece of verse you have been asked for, use the verse properly, don't make it into prose. Always have a variety of pieces and keep changing them, they quickly become stale and therefore uninteresting. If you are liked, you may be asked to do something else. Make sure you have a choice to offer up.

Be imaginative; create the character and set your scene. Find the style of your piece, particularly in something like Oscar Wilde or a late eighteenth-century play, in order to assist the director or casting director to visualise you in the period of the piece. Always imagine the person you are talking to in the scene and place them so that they become a reality for

22

you, and therefore for the director. Never talk directly to your audience unless you decide on a soliloquy. If you don't like the way you have started, you can always stop and start again.

Wear clothes to assist your character and chuck the trainers.

If you know what play is being cast you could choose a piece written in a similar style and period. You could also choose a character that has similarities. You can never be too well prepared. Don't plead lack of time, or lack of being informed as an excuse, it may be true, but nobody really cares. Most of the people you will meet are nice and wish you to succeed, so meet them with a positive attitude. Never be grim. Try to be well informed and enthusiastic about the profession.

Remember that 'many are called and few are chosen.' All you can do is to come out knowing you have done your best – no regrets.

Di Trevis

Di Trevis has directed for the Royal Shakespeare Company, the Royal National Theatre and the Royal Opera House and has run professional workshops at the Riverside Studios, London, and in France and Germany. In 1987, she directed *The Revenger's Tragedy* at the Swan Theatre in Stratford and later at the Barbican with Antony Sher in the leading role:

Let's face it. Auditioning is asking someone to love you. And they often say no. Think about this now and decide how you are going to deal with it.

Directors ask actors to perform classical pieces, such as you will find in this book, precisely because they are very difficult. Such a text will usually be of assured quality, will not yield to superficial work, and will require a mixture of technical skills in speaking, understanding and communication. Choose a piece for which you have a real affinity, one that stimulates your imagination and fills you with a feeling for the character: words you want to say. What you should aim to bring to the piece is truth, your own intuition of the character's feelings drawn from a unique experience. Yours. This will make the practised reading of the speech special and personal.

Firstly, get hold of the play from which the speech is drawn and read the *whole* play carefully with a pencil in your hand. Write down everything said about the character and everything the character says about him or herself. Look up unusual

23

words in a good dictionary which notes changes of definition at different dates. You will be amazed how words change their meanings over time. A key word written three or four centuries ago might have had quite a different resonance then.

It is part of the fascination of classical work to mine for these subtleties. Work out exactly what is being said. Then spend at least three hours actually speaking the words out loud. This seems simple until you actually do it. It is exhausting. Be careful – you must work in such a way that the words sound as if you just thought of them. This is language that needs practice and yet must never become automatic. Act out all the images until you can really see, feel and **smell** them. Say the speech in your own words. Find equivalent modern day expressions and alternate between your words and the text. Try singing the speech. Take your character out onto the streets or on a Tube journey. How would they react? If a prop is involved, never mime it. It will inform the whole speech. Find, borrow or make a substitute. Take it with you to the audition. Analyse the situation of your character previous to the speech: fighting a duel, riding a horse, hiding in a cupboard. Do it. Note all that has happened to clothes, voice, stance, mood. Get another actor to improvise with you if necessary. All this will bring a vigour and vividness to your work, a general impression of readiness of response, of fresh unblocked energy.

Even your manner of walking through the door of the interview room will be informed by proper preparation. Directors often talk of 'knowing' the moment an actor walks through the door. This is an illusion. But if an actor walks through the door with an air of readiness and an appetite to show you what he has prepared, it makes a far better impression than someone with a set of excuses lingering in the back of his mind.

Nowadays directors often like to work on a speech with the actor, suggest a new approach or ask them to use the text in a different way. If you prepare in the way I suggest you will be able to encompass new ideas, since your own work will have been through many stages and changes.

Nerves? Try improvising ahead of time a person who is calm. This helps enormously. I do it every time I face the first day in a rehearsal room. Ever thought the director might be nervous? They often are. Try putting them at their ease. Have some questions to ask – simple, practical, un-show-offy. It should be a two-way conversation. Face them calmly. Let them look at you. Breathe. Take your time to start the speech, and start again if you feel it's gone disastrously wrong. I find a false start can often be as interesting as the thing itself. When the interview is over, say goodbye cleanly and go. Actors often seem unable to leave and linger ingratiatingly, or seem to be waiting for a word or sign that one is unable to give. This always makes me sad.

An actor's life is mainly trying for jobs. It's rarely getting them. If you do, then the real horror starts: how to play the part!

Malcolm Morrison

Malcolm Morrison is Director of the Theatre Division at the Hartt School, University of Hartford, Connecticut. He is Director of the World Theatre Training Institute and Artistic Director of the Northern Stage Company. He has directed a wide range of classical plays including, most recently, *The Importance of Being Earnest*, *The Beaux' Stratagem* and *The Critic*. He lectures frequently throughout the world. His latest book, *Classical Acting*, has just been published by A & C Black in the UK.

After sitting through many auditions to find actors for classical plays I have come to the conclusion that there is one major concern in making the audition a success and that is – the ability to act. All the grooming, avoidance of 'over-done' material, expensive photographs and handsome résumés are, ultimately, no substitute for the ability to transform the audition space with well chosen material that is deeply understood and executed with a fine, but unobtrusive, technique.

I have been offered lollipops, listened to hard luck stories, and, in one case, threatened by a fifty-three year old actor with dyed blue-black hair and eyebrows – 'It's Mercutio or nothing!' he said, with both hands on the table and his face half an inch from mine. But the fact was that none of them could act.

The approach to the works of Oscar Wilde, Bernard Shaw, Shakespeare, Molière, or any of the other 'greats' of classical literature, should be just as specific and detailed in characterisation and context as to any modern realistic piece. A cursory knowledge of the play, a superficial understanding of

25

the character and an assumed attitude and voice just don't cut it. The temptation to 'play attitude' rather than the character is seductive and has to be avoided; instead there should be detailed, careful work. For example in any of the plays of Oscar Wilde the urge to play a generalised 'Upper Class English' and ignore the social context and the ability to speak long, well-constructed sentences, while maintaining a defined character, is too prevalent.

For what it is worth, my advice is: develop a strong, discreet technique, invest in the character and the play and don't offer lollipops!

Sue Parrish

Sue Parrish is Artistic Director of the Sphinx Theatre Company and Founder Director of the Women's Playhouse Trust. She won Drama Award for Best Production with Penny Casdagli's *Pardon Mr Punch* and has also directed *The Way of the World* and *The Provoked Wife*. She had this to say about playing Restoration comedy:

The most serious problem facing an actor in approaching these unjustly neglected and glorious plays is their unfamiliarity. Not only are the plays rarely performed but their world is also obscure, overshadowed by the proximity of the Elizabethan and Jacobean period.

So, in taking on a speech from a Restoration comedy, background research is vital in finding the true style. It is important to realise, for example, that the theatres had been closed for eighteen years under the Commonwealth, and, on the restoration of the monarchy, the reaction against Puritanism was embodied in a huge output of plays, and public enthusiasm for play-going.

Restoration comedy was formed in this spirit of celebration, which was expressed not simply in the comic and satiric plots, but also in the special complicity between actor and audience. The 'shared experience' of the early converted tennis-court theatres, analogous to the atmosphere at a cabaret, or the Comedy Store today, remains as a collusive flavour throughout the plays of this fifty year period. This 'complicity' is a major key to the art of playing Restoration comedy.

The opening soliloquy of 'Sir John Brute' in Vanbrugh's *Provoked Wife*, for example, is not so much direct address, not Sir John communing with himself, but more 'taking the ear' of the audience, sharing with people he assumes to be friends.

The second major key to these plays is the language. It is a complex, sophisticated language, playing with ideas, which the actor needs to deliver with relish and a certain intellectual energy. On a technical level, the lips and tongue need to be supple and under control, and the actor needs to think through every line just ahead of speaking. There is no Shakespearean 'music' to sustain emotion and energy.

Finally, there is such a sense of dangerous excitement, of breaking taboos in these plays. This 'edginess' comes from breaking the theatrical silence, making social and political commentary, but principally from bringing onto the stage the first English actresses, and thereby real sex. Women appeared as women in the public arena for the first time, way behind the rest of Europe. So the relationship between men and women is a central preoccupation of all these plays. What could be more modern than the 'proviso' scene in Congreve's *Way of the World*, with the lovers, 'Mirabell' and 'Millamant', bargaining for autonomy within marriage?

Michael Attenborough

Michael Attenborough is Executive Producer with the Royal Shakespeare Company and directed *The Changeling* at The Swan in Stratford in 1992, which afterwards transferred to the Barbican, London. He also directed David Edgar's *Pentecost* at the Young Vic in 1995.

Performing a classical piece in audition presents the actor or actress with the same challenge that would face them, were they appearing in a full-scale classical production. Namely, how to do justice to and remain truthful within formal, rich poetic language. All too often a modern actor who has come across as truthful and skilled in a contemporary piece, comes a cropper with a classical speech, largely because of a failure to meet the demands of the language. This usually takes the form of attempting to pretend that a speech in poetic language is really no different from one in contemporary speech and needs only to be approached in the same way. Such intimate 'naturalistic' acting merely results in the language sounding ridiculously high flown and so, ironically, the very striving to come across as real results in precisely the opposite.

The crucial challenge is to confront head-on the richness, sensuality and texture of poetic language and dramatic verse, and marry them together with psychological and emotional truth. My own conviction is that without fully exploring the former, you cannot achieve the later.

Sadly, one all too frequently comes across emerging drama students who have not been trained sufficiently to enable them to grapple with this central challenge when confronted by a classic text. In my opinion the majority of good young actors have an appetite for language, but have not been helped to discover how to challenge such a hunger into technical terms that will enable them to immerse themselves in the language and emerge the other side with a fully realised character. If you come in 'under' the language, it merely sounds absurd; if you come in 'over the top' of the language it will sound rhetorical, grandiose and equally ridiculous. The challenge is to come in at a level of the language so that form and content seamlessly fuse together.

Obviously you need to possess a natural instinct for such work, but I firmly believe that it is often surrounded by a needless amount of mystique and fear. I have seen many actors acquire such knowledge and technique and consequently blossom and grow as performers. The best teachers and directors can help actors and actresses to achieve this. Failing that, there are some excellent guidelines laid down in invaluable books by Cicely Berry, John Barton and Patsy Rodenberg.

The challenge is not an easy one, but in my view, with work and commitment, eminently and thrillingly achievable.

Finding a good audition speech is the first step towards a successful audition.

It is interesting to see how different the speeches in this book are by comparison with modern audition pieces – so much blood, lust, incest, intrigue and murder. There is a tremendous energy and excitement about the language, and yet not a word is over-used or out of place. There is strong drama for everybody, as well as some extremely good comedy situations. But you do have to work that bit harder on preparation – particularly on **voice**, **movement** and **background of character**.

In the early seventeenth century, playwrights Thomas Heywood and John Webster especially recommended that actors paid attention to the 'art of rhetoric'. This did not necessarily mean having a 'grandiloquent' delivery, but developing the ability to communicate well and make their voices heard in a public theatre, often with a seating capacity of two to three thousand, with audiences who weren't as polite as they are today!

Movement was also considered important and dancing was held to be a great social asset. The courtiers in the reign of James I could execute the most complicated sets of steps and capers, and by the eighteenth century the aristocracy and the 'well to do' employed dancing masters, not only to teach the latest and most fashionable dances, but also to instruct their sons and daughters in 'movement and deportment'. Restoration actors such as the great Thomas Betterton and his wife, Mary Sanderson were most meticulous about working on their characters, as indeed was Thomas Dogget, who went to such pains to perfect his 'sailor part' in *Love for Love*.

Although few of us would be prepared to go to such extremes today, we still need to do a lot more than just read the book! The New Mermaid plays, apart from giving detailed footnotes, have excellent introductions with most of the background information you need – often saving hours of research through reference libraries. They are available at most good bookshops, but there is also a tear-out order form at the back of this book.

Auditions and preparing for auditions are part of an actor's life. It is important to keep a clear head. Find out as much as you can about the part you are auditioning for and try to find a speech from the same period or something near to it. Make sure you leave plenty of time to get there – then relax. Most people are nice and want you to succeed. And above all – enjoy yourself!

CLASSICAL
AUDITION
SPEECHES

The Alchemist

Ben Jonson

First performed at the Globe Theatre, London by the King's Men in 1610, the action takes place in Lovewit's house in the City of London. Lovewit has hurried off to the country to avoid the plague, leaving his house in the sole charge of his butler, Jeremy. While his master is away, Jeremy conspires with two Jacobean low-life characters, SUBTLE, a professional alchemist and his colleague, Dol Common, to use the house to practise alchemy and various other swindles on their gullible neighbours. In this scene, Dol has just espied the wealthy Sir Epicure Mammon approaching. SUBTLE tells her to make everything ready and then prepares to meet the object of one of his most profitable swindles.

Act 1, Scene 4

SUBTLE

Face, go you, and shift.

[Exit Face]

Dol, you must presently make ready too –

... O, I did look for him

With the sun's rising: marvel, he could sleep!
This is the day, I am to perfect for him
The *magisterium*, our great work, the stone;
And yield it, made, into his hands: of which,
He has, this month, talked, as he were possessed.
And, now, he's dealing pieces on't, away.
Methinks, I see him, entering ordinaries,
Dispensing for the pox; and plaguey-houses,
Reaching his dose; walking Moorfields for lepers;
And offering citizens' wives pomander-bracelets,
As his preservative, made of the elixir;
Searching the spittle, to make old bawds young;
And the highways, for beggars, to make rich:
I see no end of his labours. He will make
Nature ashamed of her long sleep: when art,
Who's but a step-dame, shall do more, than she,
In her best love to mankind, ever could.
If his dream last, he'll turn the age, to gold.

[Exeunt]

shift change
magisterium master work
dealing ... *away* giving parts of it away (in imagination)
Reaching offering
pomander-bracelets a pomander was a perfumed ball carried as a protection against infection
(and smells)
spittle hospital

All for Love

John Dryden

The first recorded performance of this tragedy was at the Theatre Royal, Drury Lane, London, in 1677 by the King's Company. This is Dryden's version of the well-known love story of MARC ANTONY and Cleopatra, Queen of Egypt, with its central theme of conflict between overwhelming passion and duty to family and state, ending in the inevitable deaths of both lovers.

ANTONY, having lost the battle at Actium, is persuaded by his general, Ventidius, to leave Cleopatra and return to his legions waiting for him in Lower Syria. In this scene he tells Cleopatra that they must part. They have loved each other to their 'mutual ruin'. She pleads with him and he demands her silence while he attempts to explain, his speech interrupted by her further protests.

Act 2

ANTONY

You promised me your silence, and you break it
Ere I have scarce begun . . .
When I beheld you first, it was in Egypt,
Ere Caesar saw your eyes. You gave me love,
And were too young to know it: that I settled
Your father in his throne was for your sake;
I left th'acknowledgement for time to ripen.
Caesar stepped in, and with a greedy hand
Plucked the green fruit ere the first blush of red,
Yet cleaving to the bough. He was my lord,
And was, beside, too great for me to rival,
But I deserved you first, though he enjoyed you.
When, after, I beheld you in Cilicia,
An enemy to Rome, I pardoned you.
           . . . Again you break your promise.
I loved you still, and took your weak excuses,
Took you into my bosom, stained by Caesar,
And not half mine. I went to Egypt with you,
And hid me from the business of the world,
Shut out enquiring nations from my sight,
To give whole years to you.
             . . . How I loved,
Witness ye days and nights, and all your hours
That danced away with down upon your feet,
As all your business were to count my passion.
One day passed by, and nothing saw but love;
Another came, and still 'twas only love:
The suns were wearied out with looking on,
And I untired with loving.
I saw you every day, and all the day,
And every day was still but as the first,
So eager was I still to see you more.
          . . . Fulvia, my wife, grew jealous,
As she indeed had reason; raised a war
In Italy, to call me back.
          . . . While within your arms I lay,
The world fell mouldering from my hands each hour,
And left me scarce a grasp: I thank your love for't.

Arden of Faversham

Anon

The author of this tragedy remains uncertain, but it seems to have been written sometime between 1587 and 1592 and is set in Faversham, Kent. It is based on the true story of the murder of Arden, a wealthy landowner, by his young wife Alice and her lover Mosby, some forty years earlier.

After several attempts on Arden's life by hired assassins, Greene, Shakebag and BLACK WILL, Alice plans to meet her husband on his return from London, arm in arm with her lover. This will incite him to violence and she can then call for help and the assassins can come to her aid and kill him. However, the plan misfires and Shakebag and Mosby are wounded. In this scene the three assassins complain that it has never taken them so long to kill a man. BLACK WILL protests that his reputation is at stake and Arden is indeed 'preserved by a miracle'.

Scene 14

BLACK WILL

Sirrah Greene, when was I so long in killing a man? ... Thou knowest, Greene, that I have lived in London this twelve years, where I have made some go upon wooden legs for taking the wall on me; divers with silver noses for saying, 'There goes Black Will.' I have cracked as many blades as thou hast done nuts ... The bawdy-houses have paid me tribute; there durst not a whore set up unless she have agreed with me first for opening her shop windows. For a cross word of a tapster I have pierced one barrel after another with my dagger and held him by the ears till all his beer hath run out. In Thames Street a brewer's cart was like to have run over me; I made no more ado but went to the clerk and cut all the notches off his tallies and beat them about his head. I and my company have taken the constable from his watch and carried him about the fields on a coltstaff. I have broken a sergeant's head with his own mace, and bailed whom I list with my sword and buckler. All the tenpenny alehouses would stand every morning with a quart pot in their hand, saying, 'Will it please your worship drink?' He that had not done so had been sure to have had his sign pulled down and his lattice borne away the next night. To conclude, what have I not done? Yet cannot do this; doubtless he is preserved by miracle.

taking the wall i.e. taking the side of the street nearest the wall (thereby forcing Black Will into the middle of the street where it was filthiest)

silver noses i.e. false noses

tallies sticks of wood marked on one side with notches representing the amount of a debt or payment.

coltstaff (or cowlstaff): a pole used for carrying a cowl (tub).

sergeant officer responsible for arresting offenders or summoning them to court

mace staff of office

list wished, chose

tenpenny alehouses i.e. the keepers of alehouses where ale was sold for tenpence a quart.

lattice a window of lattice work painted either red or green was the sign of an alehouse.

Arden of Faversham

Anon

The author of this tragedy remains uncertain, but it seems to have been written sometime between 1587 and 1592. It is based on the true story of the murder of ARDEN, a wealthy landowner, by his young wife Alice and her lover Mosby, some forty years earlier.

ARDEN has long suspected his wife of carrying on an affair with Mosby, although the couple vehemently deny this, but has no idea of their more sinister intentions towards him. he is on his way home to Faversham, accompanied by his servant Michael and his friend, Franklin. He sends Michael to Billingsgate to check the tide for their return journey and then proceeds to tell Franklin about the horrifying dream he had the previous night.

Scene 6

ARDEN
Sirrah, get you back to Billingsgate
And learn what time the tide will serve our turn.
Come to us in Paul's. First go make the bed,
And afterwards go hearken for the flood. [*Exit Michael*]
Come, Master Franklin, you shall go with me.
This night I dreamed that being in a park,
A toil was pitched to overthrow the deer,
And I upon a little rising hill
Stood whistly watching for the herd's approach.
Even there, methoughts, a gentle slumber took me,
And summoned all my parts to sweet repose.
But in the pleasure of this golden rest
An ill-thewed foster had removed the toil,

And rounded me with that beguiling home
Which late, methought, was pitched to cast the deer.
With that he blew an evil-sounding horn,
And at the noise another herdman came
With falchion drawn, and bent it at my breast,
Crying aloud, 'Thou art the game we seek.'
With this I waked and trembled every joint,
Like one obscured in a little bush
That sees a lion foraging about,
And when the dreadful forest king is gone,
He pries about with timorous suspect
Throughout the thorny casements of the brake,
And will not think his person dangerless,
But quakes and shivers though the cause be gone.
So trust me, Franklin, when I did awake
I stood in doubt whether I waked or no,
Such great impression took this fond surprise.
God grant this vision bedeem me any good.

toil net
whistly silently
ill-thewed ill-natured
foster forester
rounded ... home trapped me with the net
cast overthrow
bent aimed
suspect apprehension
took ... surprise this foolish terror made upon me
bedeem ... good fortells no danger for me

The Atheist's Tragedy

Cyril Tourneur

This is considered to be one of the last of the revenge tragedies and was probably written in 1611. D'AMVILLE, the atheist of the title, believes that Nature is the Supreme Force and that Man is nothing more than a superior animal, children being his only claim to immortality. Wealth is therefore of prime importance as a means of making life as pleasurable as possible. To attain this end he murders his brother and arranges for his nephew to be declared dead and disinherited. He then forces a marriage between Castabella, formerly betrothed to his nephew, and Rousard, his eldest son. Towards the end of the play his world is beginning to fall apart. After discovering that his son is impotent, he lures Castabella into the churchyard at midnight, hoping to seduce her and thereby produce an heir. They are interrupted by his nephew, who leaps out at him disguised as a ghost.

In this scene he is wandering distractedly through the churchyard and 'starts at the sight of a death's head'.

Act 4, Scene 3

D'AMVILLE
Why dost thou stare upon me? Thou art not
The skull of him I murdered. What has thou
To do to vex my conscience? Sure thou wert
The head of a most dogged usurer,
Th'art so uncharitable. And that bawd,
The sky there, she could shut the windows and
The doors of this great chamber of the world,
And draw the curtains of the clouds between
Those lights and me about this bed of earth,

When that same strumpet, Murder, and myself
Committed sin together. Then she could
Leave us i' th' dark till the close deed
Was done, but now that I begin to feel
The loathsome horror of my sin and, like
A lecher emptied of his lust, desire
To bury my face under my eyebrows and
Would steal from my shame unseen, she meets me
I' th' face with all her light corrupted eyes
To challenge payment o' me. O behold!
Yonder's the ghost of old Montferrers in
A long white sheet, climbing yond' lofty mountain
To complain to Heav'n of me. Montferrers!
'Pox o' fearfulness. 'Tis nothing but
A fair white cloud. Why, was I born a coward?
He lies that says so. Yet the countenance of
A bloodless worm might ha' the courage now
To turn my blood to water. The trembling motion
Of an aspen leaf would make me, like
The shadow of that leaf, lie shaking under 't.
I could now commit a murder, were
It but to drink the fresh warm blood of him
I murdered, to supply the want and weakness
O' mine own, 'tis grown so cold and phlegmatic ...
Mountains o'erwhelm me – the ghost of old Montferrers
haunts me ...
O were my body circumvolved
Within that cloud, that when the thunder tears
His passage open, it might scatter me
To nothing in the air!

Bartholmew Fair

Ben Jonson

This Jacobean comedy was first performed in 1614 by the Lady Elizabeth's Servants at the Hope Theatre, London. It is a lively festive entertainment with no central hero, but no fewer than thirty-four characters. These range from minor landed gentry to the 'common folk' who come to visit the fair, and the stall holders themselves, the entertainers, cut-purses and swindlers.

In this opening scene, the Proctor, JOHN LITTLEWIT, and his wife, Win, are getting ready to go to the fair. LITTLEWIT 'has a stitch new fallen in his black silk stocking'* which he attends to. His wife Win comes in to show him her new finery.

_____

* as explained in the Introduction at the beginning of the play

Act 1, Scene 1

LITTLEWIT
A pretty conceit, and worth the finding! I ha' such luck to spin out these fine things still, and like a silk-worm, out of myself. Here's Master Bartholomew Cokes, of Harrow o'th'Hill, i'th'County of Middlesex, Esquire, takes forth his licence to marry Mistress Grace Wellborn of the said place and county. And when does he take it forth? Today! The four-and-twentieth of August! Bartholmew day! Bartholmew upon Bartholmew! There's the device! Who would have marked such a leap-frog chance now? A very less than ames-ace on two dice! Well, go thy ways, John Littlewit, Proctor John Littlewit – one o' the pretty wits o' Paul's, the Little Wit of London, so thou art called, and something beside. When a quirk or a quiblin does scape thee, and thou dost not watch, and apprehend it, and bring it afore the constable of conceit – there now. I speak quib too – let 'em carry

42

thee out o' the Archdeacon's court into his kitchen, and make a Jack
of thee, instead of a John. there I am again, la!

[*Enter to him* Win]

Win, good morrow, Win. Aye, marry, Win! Now you look finely
indeed, Win! This cap does convince! You'd not ha' worn it, Win, nor
ha' had it velvet, but a rough country beaver with a copper band,
like the coney-skin woman of Budge Row? Sweet Win, let me kiss it!
And her fine high shoes, like the Spanish lady! Good Win, go a little; I would fain see thee pace, pretty Win! By this fine cap, I could
never leave kissing on't . . . Is there the proctor, or doctor indeed, i'
the diocese, that ever had the fortune to win him such a Win? – There
I am again! – I do feel conceits coming upon me more than I am able
to turn tongue to. A pox o' these pretenders to wit! your Three
Cranes, Mitre, and Mermaid men! Not a corn of true salt nor a grain
of right mustard amongst them all. They may stand for places or so,
again the next witfall, and pay twopence in a quart more for their
canary than other men. But gi' me the man can start up a Justice of
Wit out of six-shillings beer, and give the law to all the poets and
poet-suckers i' town! Because they are the players' gossips? 'Slid,
other men have wives as fine as the players', and as well dressed.
Come hither, Win.

[*Kisses her*]

device clever design

leap-frog chance chance of two interchange-
able things appearing together

very less truly slighter (with the word
'chance' understood)

ames-ace ambs-ace, double ace, lowest
possible throw with two dice

quirk quip

quiblin quibble, pun

conceit wit

Jack mechanical device for turning the spit
when roasting meat

does convince is overwhelming, is a knock-
out

beaver hat made of beaver's fur

coney-skin woman woman who sells rabbit-
skins

kiss it kiss you (baby language)

go walk

on't you (literally 'of it')

corn grain

salt . . . mustard sharp pungent wit

stand for strive for

again in anticipation of

witfall the letting-fall of a jest or repartee

canary light sweet wine from the Canary
Islands

six-shillings beer small beer sold at six
shillings a barrel

poet-suckers sucking poets, fledgling poets

gossips familiar acquaintances

'Slid by God's eyelid

43

The Beaux' Stratagem

George Farquhar

First performed in 1707 at the Queen's Theatre, Haymarket, London, by Her Majesty's Sworn Comedians and set in Lichfield. The main action concerns the adventures of the two beaux, Aimwell and Archer, who travel up to Lichfield from London to recoup their 'broken fortune'. They put up at a local inn and among other guests they meet CAPTAIN GIBBET, a military looking gentleman, who turns out to be a highwayman in league with the Landlord and his daughter, Cherry.

In this scene GIBBET has just robbed the London stage-coach and returns to the inn with his spoils. He hands them over to Cherry for safe keeping, giving her a pot of rouge for herself, stolen from a high-born lady.

Act 2, Scene 2

GIBBET

Landlord, landlord, is the coast clear? ... No matter, ask no questions, all fair and honourable. – Here, my dear Cherry. [*Gives her a bag*] Two hundred sterling pounds, as good as any that ever hanged or saved a rogue; lay 'em by with the rest; and here – three wedding or mourning rings, 'tis much the same, you know. – Here, two silver-hilted swords; I took those from fellows that never show any part of their swords but the hilts. Here is a diamond necklace which the lady hid in the privatest place in the coach, but I found it out. This gold watch I took from a pawnbroker's wife; it was left in her hands by a person of quality: there's the arms upon the case ... who had I the money from? Ah! poor woman! I pitied her; – from a poor lady just eloped from her husband. She had made up her cargo, and was bound for Ireland as hard as she could drive; she told me of her husband's barbarous usage, and so I left her half a crown. But I had almost forgot, my dear Cherry; I have a present for you ... A pot of ceruse, my child, that I took out of a lady's underpocket ... I'm sure the lady that I took it from had a coronet upon her handkerchief. – Here, take my cloak, and go, secure the premises.

mourning rings rings worn in memory of the dead
ceruse a white-lead cosmetic
premises the articles previously mentioned

The Beaux' Stratagem

George Farquhar

First performed in 1707 at the Queen's Theatre, Haymarket, London by Her Majesty's Sworn Comedians and set in Lichfield. The main action concerns the adventures of the two beaux, Aimwell and Archer, who travel up to Lichfield from London in the guise of Viscount and Footman, to recoup their 'broken fortune'.

On Archer's suggestion they attend the local church and the Squire's sister, Dorinda, falls in love with Aimwell at first sight. Dorinda and her sister-in-law, Mrs Sullen, send their much put-upon servant, SCRUB, to find out all he can about the two strangers. In this scene he returns to give his 'packet of news' to the ladies.

Act 3, Scene 1

SCRUB

Madam, I have brought you a packet of news ... In the first place, I inquired who the gentleman was; they told me, he was a stranger. Secondly, I asked what the gentleman was; they answered and said, that they never saw him before. Thirdly, I inquired what countryman he was; they replied, 'twas more than they knew. Fourthly, I demanded whence he came; their answer was, they could not tell. And, fifthly, I asked whither he went, and they replied, they knew nothing of the matter – and this is all I could learn ... some think he's a spy, some guess he's a mountebank; some say one thing, some another; but, for my own part, I believe he's a Jesuit ... Because he keeps his horses always ready saddled, and his footman talks French ... Ay, he and the count's footman were gabbering French like two intriguing ducks in a mill-pond; and I believe they talked of me, for they laughed consumedly ... The footman? Lord, madam, I took him for a captain, he's so bedizened with lace. And then he has tops to his shoes, up to his mid leg, a silver-headed cane dangling at his knuckles; he carries his hands in his pockets just so – [*Walks in the French air*] – and has a fine long periwig tied up in a bag. – Lord, madam, he's clear another sort of man than I!

mountebank itinerant quack
gabbering talking volubly, jabbering
tops uppermost part of the leg of a high-boot or riding-boot
bag small silken pouch to contain the back-hair of a wig

The Broken Heart

John Ford

Possibly published in 1633 and performed in a private house in Blackfriars, London, it is set in Sparta. Penthea, in love with Orgilus, has been forced to marry BASSANES, a rich nobleman, by her brother Ithocles. BASSANES, insanely jealous and aware of her former attachment to Orgilus, keeps her shut up at home with an old serving woman to watch over her. In this scene, BASSANES orders his servant to have the window overlooking the street boarded up, so that passers by cannot see in or communicate with Penthea in any way at all.

Act 1, Scene 3

BASSANES
I'll have that window next the street dammed up;
It gives too full a prospect to temptation,
And courts a gazer's glances. There's a lust
Committed by the eye, that sweats and travails,
Plots, wakes, contrives, till the deformed bear-whelp
Adultery be licked into the act,
The very act. That light shall be dammed up;
D'ee hear, sir?
                                        . . . a mason
Shall be provided . . .
                                        . . . Some rogue,
Some rogue of your confederacy, (factor
For slaves and strumpets) to convey close packets
From this spruce springal and the tother youngster,
That gaudy earwig, or my lord your patron,
Whose pensioner you are. – I'll tear thy throat out,
Son of a cat, ill-looking hound's-head, rip up

Thy ulcerous maw, if I but scent a paper,
A scroll, but half as big as what can cover
A wart upon thy nose, a spot, a pimple,
Directed to my lady. It may prove
A mystical preparative to lewdness . . .
The city housewives, cunning in the traffic
Of chamber-merchandise, set all at price
By wholesale; yet they wipe their mouths and simper,
Cull, kiss, and cry 'sweetheart', and stroke the head
Which they have branched; and all is well again.
Dull clods of dirt, who dare not feel the rubs
Stuck on their foreheads.
                              . . . Dames at court,
Who flaunt in riots, run another bias.
Their pleasure heaves the patient ass that suffers
Up on the stilts of office, titles, incomes;
Promotion justifies the shame, and sues for't.
Poor honour, thou art stabbed, and bleedest to death
By such unlawful hire. The country mistress
Is yet more wary, and in blushes hides
Whatever trespass draws her troth to guilt.
But all are false. On this truth I am bold:
No woman but can fall, and doth, or would. –
Now for the newest news about the city;
What blab the voices, sirrah?

light window
suddenly immediately
factor agent
close packets secret letters
springal youth
earwig flatterer
mystical secret
housewives hussies
Cull embrace
branched horned
bias indirect course
mewed shed (used of a bird moulting)

Bussy D'Ambois

George Chapman

This tragedy was probably written in 1604 for the Children of
the Chapel Royal, who were later to become the Children of the
Queen's Revels.

BUSSY D'AMBOIS is an historical figure, well known at the
time for his political activities and amours at the Court of the
French King Henry III. In the play he is likened to Hercules –
brave, heroic and anxious to serve his King, but he is also blunt
and outspoken, making many enemies. In this opening scene,
BUSSY is poor and dressed in shabby attire. He is discontented
in a world where Fortune only 'rules the state of things'.

Act 1, Scene 1

BUSSY

Fortune, not Reason, rules the state of things,
Reward goes backwards, Honour on his head;
Who is not poor, is monstrous; only Need
Gives form and worth to every human seed.
As cedars beaten with incessant storms,
So great men flourish; and do imitate
Unskilful statuaries, who suppose,
In forging a Colossus, if they make him
Straddle enough, strut, and look big, and gape,
Their work is goodly: so our tympanous statists
In their affected gravity of voice,
Sourness of countenance, manners' cruelty,
Authority, wealth, and all the spawn of Fortune,
Think they bear all the kingdom's worth before them;
Yet differ not from those colossic statues,
Which, with heroic forms without o'er-spread,

Within are nought but mortar, flint, and lead.
Man is a torch borne in the wind; a dream
But of a shadow, summed with all his substance;
And as great seamen, using all their powers
And skills in Neptune's deep invisible paths,
In tall ships richly built and ribbed with brass,
To put a girdle round about the world,
When they have done it, coming near their haven,
Are glad to give a warning-piece, and call
A poor staid fisherman, that never passed
His country's sight, to waft and guide them in;
So when we wander furthest through the waves
Of glassy Glory and the gulfs of State,
Topt with all titles, spreading all our reaches,
As if each private arm would sphere the world,
We must to Virtue for her guide resort,
Or we shall shipwrack in our safest port.

                                    [*He lies down.*]

on his head upside down
Need poverty
statuaries makers of statues
give a warning-piece fire a signal gun
waft convey safely
spreading . . . reaches putting on all canvas

The Changeling

Thomas Middleton and William Rowley

First produced in 1622 at the Phoenix Theatre in Drury Lane, London, and performed by the Lady Elizabeth's Players, it is set in Alicante on the east coast of Spain. DE FLORES, servant to the Governor of Alicante, has long desired and lusted after his master's beautiful daughter, Beatrice Joanna, even though he knows she detests his 'ugly dog-face' and cannot bear him near her. She is betrothed to Alonzo de Piracquo, but has fallen deeply in love with the nobleman Alsemero. As the marriage day draws nearer she becomes more and more desperate and despite her loathing for DE FLORES, hires him to kill Alonzo. In this scene DE FLORES comes to claim his reward, bearing with him the finger of Alonzo with Beatrice's ring still on it. Beatrice tells him to bury the finger and keep the ring, offering him in addition three thousand golden florins. He is contemptuous of the money. The killing of Alonzo has made them one and he demands that she surrenders her body to him or he will divulge her part in the murder.

Act 3, Scene 4

DE FLORES

                                    . . . I have eased you
Of your trouble; think on't. I'm in pain
And must be eased of you; 'tis a charity.
Justice invites your blood to understand me.
                                    . . . Soft, lady, soft!
The last is not yet paid for. O, this act
Has put me into spirit: I was as greedy on't
As the parched earth of moisture, when the clouds weep.
Did you not mark, I wrought myself into't,
Nay, sued and kneeled for't? Why was all that pains took?

You see I have thrown contempt upon your gold:
Not that I want it [not], for I do piteously –
In order I will come unto't, and make use on't –
But 'twas not held so precious to begin with,
For I place wealth after the heels of pleasure;
And were I not resolved in my belief
That thy virginity were perfect in thee,
I should but take my recompense with grudging,
As if I had but half my hopes I agreed for . . .
Look but into your conscience, read me there;
'Tis a true book, you'll find me there your equal.
Push, fly not to your birth, but settle you
In what the act has made you; y'are no more now.
You must forget your parentage to me:
Y'are the deed's creature; by that name you lost
Your first condition; and I challenge you
As peace and innocency has turned you out
And made you one with me . . .
Yes, my fair murd'ress. Do you urge me,
Though thou writ'st 'maid', thou whore in thy affection?
'Twas changed from thy first love, and that's a kind
Of whoredom in thy heart; and he's changed now
To bring thy second on, thy Alsemero,
Whom (by all sweets that ever darkness tasted)
If I enjoy thee not, thou ne'er enjoy'st:
I'll blast the hopes and joys of marriäge –
I'll cónfess all; my life I rate at nothing . . .
She that in life and love refuses me,
In death and shame my partner she shall be.

pain i.e. of sexual desire

eased sexually relieved (of = by)

charity (here) a gift to someone sexually deprived

Soft i.e. not so fast

act i.e. of blood

me . . . spirit Read 'm'nto spir't'.

spirit (thought to be produced by blood) animation; sexual desire

In order in due course

pleasure sexual pleasure

equal i.e. in violence, and hence in other respects

by . . . condition having adopted the name of Murderer, you have lost the original innocence of Eve and your parenthood

challenge lay claim to

turned you out i.e. from Paradise and your family

urge provoke

affection passionate desire

changed i.e. from life to death

bring on introduce and advance, with play on 'excite sexually'

sweets pleasures of sexual intimacy

The Country Wife

William Wycherley

First performed in 1675, probably at the Theatre Royal, Drury Lane, London, by the King's Company. JACK PINCHWIFE, a middle aged rake, has married Margery, a pretty young country girl, and is determined to keep her away from the young 'gallants' about town. When he discovers that the notorious Master Horner has been paying attentions to her and has even kissed her, he orders his young wife to sit down and write to Horner telling him that she wants nothing more to do with him. However, Margery is determined secretly to continue her 'romance'.

In this scene, PINCHWIFE enters to find Margery once more at her writing desk. She tries to run out of the room, but he stops her, snatches away the letter she has been writing and starts to read it. It is a love letter to her 'Dear Master Horner . . .'

Act 4, Scene 4

PINCHWIFE

What, writing more letters? . . . How's this! Nay, you shall not stir, madam. 'Dear, dear, dear Master Horner' – very well! – I have taught you to write letters to good purpose – but let's see't – 'First, I am to beg your pardon for my boldness in writing to you, which I'd have you to know I would not have done, had not you said first you loved me so extremely, which if you do, you will never suffer me to lie in the arms of another man, whom I loathe, nauseate, and detest' – Now you can write these filthy words! But what follows? – 'Therefore I hope you will speedily find some way to free me from this unfortunate match, which was never, I assure you, of my choice, but I'm afraid 'tis already too far gone. However, if you love me, as I do you, you will try what you can do, but you must help me away before tomorrow, or else, alas, I shall be for ever out of your reach, for I can defer no longer our' – [*The letter concludes*] 'Our'? What is to follow 'our'? Speak, what? Our journey into the country I suppose? Oh, woman, damned woman! And love, damned love, their old tempter! For this is one of his miracles. In a moment he can make those blind that could see, and those see that were blind, those dumb that could speak, and those prattle who were dumb before; nay, what is more than all, make these dough-baked, senseless, indocile animals, women, too hard for us, their politic lords and rulers, in a moment. But make an end of your letter and then I'll make and end of you thus, and all my plagues together.

[*Draws his sword*]

match This usually means an engagement rather than a marriage; seems a bit disingenuous
dough-baked half-baked
indocile hard to teach
politic lawful

The Critic

Richard Brinsley Sheridan

First performed at Drury Lane, London, in 1799, this comedy of
manners is set in London and satirises plays of romantic love
and political excess.

The action revolves around the forthcoming production of *The
Spanish Armada* written and directed by the entrepreneurial MR
PUFF. In this scene PUFF has called on theatre critic, Dangle,
and his friend, Sneer, to invite them to a rehearsal of his new
tragi-drama. In the course of conversation, Sneer inquires how
he started out on his literary career and PUFF launches into this
bizarre account of his early ventures into journalism.

Act 1, Scene 2

PUFF

Egad Sir, – sheer necessity – the proper parent of an art so nearly
allied to invention: you must know Mr Sneer, that from the first time
I tried my hand at an advertisement, my success was such, that for
some time after, I led a most extraordinary life indeed! ... Sir, I
supported myself two years entirely by my misfortunes ... Yes Sir,
assisted by long sickness, and other occasional disorders; and a very
comfortable living I had of it ... Harkee! – By advertisements – 'To
the charitable and humane!' and 'to those whom Providence hath
blessed with affluence!' ... And in truth, I deserved what I got, for
I suppose never man went through such a series of calamities in the
same space of time! – Sir, I was five times made a bankrupt, and
reduced from a state of affluence, by a train of unavoidable misfortunes! then Sir, though a very industrious tradesman, I was twice
burnt out, and lost my little all, both times! – I lived upon those fires
a month. – I soon after was confined by a most excruciating disorder,
and lost the use of my limbs! – That told very well, for I had the case

56

strongly attested, and went about to collect the subscriptions myself
... – In November last? – O no! – I was at that time a close prisoner
in the Marshalsea, for a debt benevolently contracted to serve a
friend! – I was afterwards twice tapped for a dropsy, which declined
into a very profitable consumption! – I was then reduced to – O no
– then I became a widow with six helpless children, – after having
had eleven husbands pressed, and being left every time eight months
gone with child, and without money to get me into an hospital! ...
Why, yes, – though I made some occasional attempts at felo de se;
but as I did not find those *rash actions* answer, I left off killing myself
very soon. – Well, Sir, – at last, what with bankruptcies, fires, gouts,
dropsies, imprisonments, and other valuable calamities, having got
together a pretty handsome sum, I determined to quit a business
which had always gone rather against my conscience, and in a more
liberal way still to indulge my talents for fiction and embellishment,
through my favourite channels of diurnal communication – and so,
Sir, you have my history.

Marshalsea the debtors' prison on the south bank of the Thames

tapped for a dropsy The watery fluid collecting in the body tissues of a patient suffering from
dropsy has to be drained off.

pressed press-ganged into the navy

felo de se suicide

channels of diurnal communication daily newspapers

The Double-Dealer

William Congreve

This Restoration comedy was first performed in 1693 at the Theatre Royal, London, by Their Majesties' Servants and is set in a Gallery in Lord Touchwood's House on the eve of the wedding of his nephew, MELLEFONT, and Sir Paul Plyant's daughter, Cynthia.

The main story centres on the plot against MELLEFONT by his 'double dealing' friend, Maskwell and his Aunt, the dangerous Lady Touchwood. She is in love with MELLEFONT and determined to do anything within her power to prevent the marriage. In this scene, MELLEFONT describes to his friend, Careless, his extraordinary confrontation with his Aunt and his conviction that she intends to ruin him.

Act 1, Scene 1

MELLEFONT

. . . You shall judge whether I have not reason to be alarmed. None besides you and Maskwell are acquainted with the secret of my Aunt Touchwood's violent passion for me. Since my first refusal of her addresses, she has endeavoured to do me all ill offices with my uncle; yet has managed 'em with that subtlety that to him they have borne the face of kindness; while her malice, like a dark lantern, only shone upon me, where it was directed. Still it gave me less perplexity to prevent the success of her displeasure, than to avoid the importunities of her love; and of two evils, I thought myself favoured in her aversion: but whether urged by her despair, and the short prospect of time she saw to accomplish her designs; whether the hopes of revenge, or of her love, terminated in the view of this my marriage with Cynthia, I know not; but this morning she surprised me in my bed. – . . . What at first amazed me; for I looked to have seen her in all the transports of a slighted and revengeful woman: but when I expected thunder from her voice, and lightning in her eyes, I saw her melted into tears, and hushed into a sigh. It was long before either of us spoke, passion had tied her tongue, and amazement mine. – In short, the consequence was thus, she omitted nothing that the most violent love could urge, or tender words express; which when she saw had no effect, but still I pleaded honour and nearness of blood to my uncle, then came the storm I feared at first: for starting from my bedside like a fury, she flew to my sword, and with much ado I prevented her doing me or herself a mischief: having disarmed her, in a gust of passion she left me, and in a resolution, confirmed by a thousand curses, not to close her eyes, till she had seen my ruin.

The Double-Dealer

William Congreve

This Restoration comedy was first performed in 1693 at the Theatre Royal, London, by Their Majesties' Servants and is set in Lord Touchwood's House on the eve of the wedding of his nephew, Mellefont, and Sir Paul Plyant's daughter, Cynthia.

The main story centres on the plot against Mellefont by his 'double dealing friend' MASKWELL, himself in love with Cynthia, and his Aunt, the dangerous Lady Touchwood. On MASKWELL'S suggestion, Lady Touchwood has persuaded Sir Paul's wife, a foolish coquette who believes that every young man is attracted to her, that Mellefont is in love with her. Lady Plyant in turn tells her husband, who immediately forbids the marriage and whisks Cynthia away with him. MASKWELL consoles Mellefont, telling him he has his best interests at heart and that everything will be well again before morning. Alone on stage MASKWELL boasts of his 'dear dissimulation' and reveals his plans to marry Cynthia and gain her inheritance.

Act 2

MASKWELL

Till then, success will attend me; for when I meet you, I meet the only obstacle to my fortune. Cynthia, let thy beauty gild my crimes; and whatsoever I commit of treachery or deceit shall be imputed to me as a merit. – Treachery! What treachery? Love cancels all the bonds of friendship, and sets men right upon their first foundations.

Duty to kings, piety to parents, gratitude to benefactors, and fidelity to friends, are different and particular ties: but the name of 'rival' cuts 'em all asunder, and is a general acquittance – rival is equal, and love like death an universal leveller of mankind. Ha! But is there not such a thing as honesty? Yes, and whosoever has it about him bears an enemy in his breast: for your honest man, as I take it, is that nice, scrupulous, conscientious person who will cheat nobody but himself; such another coxcomb as your wise man, who is too hard for all the world, and will be made a fool of by nobody, but himself: ha, ha, ha. Well, for wisdom and honesty, give me cunning and hypocrisy; oh 'tis such a pleasure to angle for fair-faced fools! Then that hungry gudgeon Credulity will bite at anything. – Why, let me see, I have the same face, the same words and accents, when I speak what I do think, and when I speak what I do not think – the very same – and dear dissimulation is the only art not to be known from nature.

> Why will mankind be fools, and be deceived?
> And why friends' and lovers' oaths believed?
> When each, who searches strictly his own mind,
> May so much fraud and power of baseness find.

> > [*Exit*]

Dr Faustus

Christopher Marlowe

Possibly first performed in 1594, several months after the play-wright's assassination. It is a tragedy of damnation. FAUSTUS sells his soul to the Devil in return for twenty–four years of knowledge, pleasure and power. His is the sin of pride with its inevitable downfall.

At the beginning of the play we see FAUSTUS sitting discontented in his study. He has vast knowledge, fame and popularity, but he is still only 'man'. He rejects his study of law and medicine, which can only restore health not life, and turns to magic. In this scene he has conjured up, or thinks he has conjured up, Mephastophilis in the shape of a Franciscan friar. Mephastophilis explains that he is one of the 'unhappy spirits that fell with Lucifer' and begs FAUSTUS to 'leave these frivolous demands'. But FAUSTUS refuses to listen and sends him back to bargain with Lucifer, swearing that he will surrender up his soul.

Act 1, Scene 3

FAUSTUS
What, is great Mephastophilis so passionate
For being deprived of the joys of heaven?
Learn thou of Faustus manly fortitude,
And scorn those joys thou never shalt possess.
Go bear these tidings to great Lucifer,
Seeing Faustus hath incurred eternal death
By desperate thoughts against Jove's deity:
Say, he surrenders up to him his soul
So he will spare him four and twenty years,
Letting him live in all voluptuousness,
Having thee ever to attend on me,
To give me whatsoever I shall ask,
To tell me whatsoever I demand,
To slay mine enemies, and aid my friends,
And always be obedient to my will.
Go, and return to mighty Lucifer,
And meet me in my study at midnight,
And then resolve me of thy master's mind . . .
Had I as many souls as there be stars
I'd give them all for Mephastophilis.
By him I'll be great emperor of the world,
And make a bridge through the moving air
To pass the ocean with a band of men;
I'll join the hills that bind the Afric shore,
And make that land continent to Spain,
And both contributory to my crown.
The emperor shall not live but by my leave,
Nor any potentate of Germany.
Now that I have obtained what I desire
I'll live in speculation of this art
Till Mephastophilis return again.

The Duchess of Malfi

John Webster

The first performance was most probably sometime between 1612 and 1614, being presented in London privately at Blackfriars and publicly at the Globe. It is set mainly in Malfi and in Rome and concerns the tragedy that follows the liaison and subsequent marriage of the Duchess of Malfi and her steward Antonio, and the jealousy of her two brothers – one the Cardinal and the other her twin, FERDINAND – who hire the devilish Bosola to spy on her and eventually murder her.

In this scene the Duchess has been strangled and FERDINAND asks Bosola to show him her body.

Act 4, Scene 2

FERDINAND
                              ... She and I were twins:
And should I die this instant, I had liv'd
Her time to a minute ...
                              ... Let me see her face again;
Why didst not thou pity her? What an excellent
Honest man might'st thou have been
If thou hadst borne her to some sanctuary!
Or, bold in a good cause, oppos'd thyself
With thy advanced sword above thy head,
Between her innocence and my revenge!
I bad thee, when I was distracted of my wits,
Go kill my dearest friend, and thou hast done't.
For let me but examine well the cause;
What was the meanness of her match to me?
Only I must confess, I had a hope,
Had she continu'd widow, to have gain'd
An infinite mass of treasure by her death:
And that was the main cause; her marriage,
That drew a stream of gall quite through my heart;
For thee, (as we observe in tragedies
That a good actor many times is curs'd
For playing a villain's part) I hate thee for't:
And, for my sake, say thou hast done much ill, well ...
By what authority didst thou execute
This bloody sentence?
                              [*By yours.*]

Mine? Was I her judge?
Did any ceremonial form of law
Doom her to not-being? did a complete jury
Deliver her conviction up i'th' court?
Where shalt thou find this judgement register'd
Unless in hell? See: like a bloody fool
Th'hast forfeited thy life, and thou shalt die for't.

---

approv'd confirmed, demonstrated

65

Eastward Ho!

Ben Jonson, George Chapman & John Marston

This Jacobean city comedy seems to have been first performed in 1605 at Blackfriars, London, by the Children of Her Majesty's Revels, and is the result of the successful collaboration of three well-known and respected playwrights. 'Eastward Ho!' was the cry of the Thames boatmen to hail passengers going down the river to Greenwich, that is towards the Court and the prospect of adventure and 'easy gold'. The action centres around TOUCHSTONE, a Goldsmith, whose belief in the old order of society where hard work, thrift and honesty win out in the end, is derided by his apprentice Quicksilver and his eldest daughter, the haughty Gertrude. In this scene a Page arrives to announce that Sir Petronel Flash, the knight who is courting his daughter, is about to pay him a visit.

Act 1, Scene 1

TOUCHSTONE

To make up the match with my eldest daughter, my wife's dilling, whom she longs to call madam. He shall find me unwillingly ready, boy.

[*Exit Page*]

There's another affliction too. As I have two prentices, the one of a boundless prodigality, the other of a most hopeful industry; so have I only two daughters: the eldest, of a proud ambition and nice wantonness, the other of a modest humility and comely soberness. The one must be ladyfied, forsooth, and be attired just to the court-cut and long-tail. So far she is ill-natured to the place and means of my preferment and fortune, that she throws all the contempt and despite hatred itself can cast upon it. Well, a piece of land she has, 'twas her grandmother's gift: let her, and her Sir Petronel, flash out that! But as for my substance, she that scorns me, as I am a citizen and tradesman, shall never pamper her pride with my industry; shall never use me as men do foxes: keep themselves warm in the skin, and throw the body that bare it to the dunghill. I must go entertain this Sir Petronel. Golding, my utmost care's for thee, and only trust in thee; look to the shop. As for you, Master Quicksilver, think of husks, for thy course is running directly to the Prodigals' hogs' trough! Husks, sirrah! 'Work upon that now'!

dilling darling
nice lascivious, loose
give arms bear arms, display one's gentlemanly rank

Edward the Second

Christopher Marlowe

Probably first performed in the last few months of 1592 by the Earl of Pembroke's Company and published shortly after Marlowe's death.

Edward the Second is a weak and foolish king, whose infatuation for the courtier, PIERCE DE GAVESTON, angers the barons and brings about his eventual downfall and horrifying death.

GAVESTON, banished from the kingdom by Edward's father, has been living in exile in France. Now the old King is dead and Edward has summoned back his 'favourite' to share his kingdom with him. In this opening scene, GAVESTON has just arrived back in England and meets 'Three Poor Men' coming to beg favours of him. He dismisses them and in this speech outlines his plans for a future of lascivious pleasures in the company of his beloved Monarch.

Act 1, Scene 1

GAVESTON

... These are not men for me;
I must have wanton poets, pleasant wits,
Musicians, that with touching of a string
May draw the pliant king which way I please;
Music and poetry is his delight,
Therefore I'll have Italian masques by night,
Sweet speeches, comedies and pleasing shows,
And in the day when he shall walk abroad,
Like sylvan nymphs my pages shall be clad,
My men like satyrs grazing on the lawns
Shall with their goat feet dance an antic hay;
Sometime a lovely boy in Dian's shape,
With hair that gilds the water as it glides,
Crownets of pearl about his naked arms,
And in his sportful hands an olive-tree
To hide those parts which men delight to see,
Shall bathe him in a spring, and there hard by
One like Actaeon peeping through the grove
Shall by the angry goddess be transformed,
And running in the likeness of an hart,
By yelping hounds pulled down and seem to die;
Such things as these best please his majesty.
My lord! Here comes the king and the nobles
From the parliament; I'll stand aside.

Epicoene *or* The Silent Woman

Ben Jonson

First performed by the Children of Her Majestie's Revels most probably in 1609 and described in Jonson's own words as 'a comedy of affliction'. Nearly every character is 'epicene' in some way or other, and the Silent Woman of the title herself turns out to be a man by the end of the play.

The action centres around MOROSE, an elderly man obsessed with the need for absolute silence, who decides to marry only because he wishes to disinherit his nephew, and has even gone to the extent of employing someone to find him a dumb woman, whose silence will be 'dowry enough'.

We see MOROSE for the first time in this scene, giving orders to his servant, Mute, and insisting that his replies are in dumb show only.

Act 2, Scene 1

MOROSE

Cannot I yet find out a more compendious method than by this trunk to save my servants the labour of speech and mine ears the discord of sounds? Let me see. All discourses but mine own afflict me, they seem harsh, impertinent, and irksome. Is it not possible that thou shouldst answer me by signs, and I apprehend thee, fellow? Speak not, though I question you. You have taken the ring off from the street door, as I bade you? Answer me not by speech but by silence, unless it be otherwise. – Very good.

[*At the breaches, still the fellow makes legs or signs*]
And you have fastened on a thick quilt or flock-bed on the outside of the door, that if they knock with their daggers or with brickbats, they can make no noise? But with your leg, your answer, unless it be otherwise. – Very good. This is not only fit modesty in a servant,

but good state and discretion in a master. And you have been with Cutbeard, the barber, to have him come to me? – Good. And he will come presently? Answer me not but with your leg, unless it be otherwise; if it be otherwise, shake your head or shrug. – [*Mute makes a leg*] So. Your Italian and Spaniard are wise in these, and it is a frugal and comely gravity. How long will it be ere Cutbeard come? Stay, if an hour, hold up your whole hand; if half an hour, two fingers; if a quarter, one. – [*Mute holds up one finger bent*] Good; half a quarter? 'Tis well. And have you given him a key to come in without knocking? – Good. And is the lock oiled, and the hinges, today? – Good. And the quilting of the stairs nowhere worn out and bare? – Very good. I see by much doctrine and impulsion, it may be effected. Stand by. The Turk in this divine discipline is admirable, exceeding all the potentates of the earth; still waited on by mutes, and all his commands so executed, yea, even in the war, as I have heard, and in his marches, most of his charges and directions given by signs and with silence: an exquisite art! And I am heartily ashamed and angry oftentimes that the princes of Christendom should suffer a barbarian to transcend 'em in so high a point of felicity. I will practise it hereafter.

[*One winds a horn without*]

How now? Oh! oh! What villain, what prodigy of mankind is that? – Look. [*Exit Mute. Horn sounds again*] – Oh! cut his throat, cut his throat! What murderer, hell-hound, devil can this be?

compendious expeditious, direct
impertinent irrelevant
ring (circular) door-knocker
flock-bed mattress stuffed with wool or cotton waste
brickbats pieces of brick
state dignity of demeanour
discretion judgement
doctrine teaching (Latin *doctrina*)
impulsion influence, instigation
by to one side
discipline branch of instruction
charges . . . directions orders . . . instructions for the deployment of troops
prodigy monster

Gammer Gurton's Needle

Mr S.

This sixteenth-century comedy was first performed at Christ's College, Cambridge sometime between the 1550s and 1560s and is attributed to a Mr S. – Master of Arts. Gammer Gurton has lost her needle and, unable to finish sewing her man Hodge's breeches, has the whole house turned upside down looking for it. In this scene her houseboy COCK comes out to tell her how Hodge is progressing in his search, describing him raking through the ashes and then chasing Gib the cat upstairs.

Act 1, Scene 5

COCK

Gog's cross, Gammer, if ye will laugh, look in but at the door,
And see how Hodge lieth tumbling and tossing amidst the floor,
Raking there some fire to find among the ashes dead
Where there is not one spark so big as a pin's head.
At last, in a dark corner, two sparks he thought he sees,
Which were indeed nought else but Gib our cat's two eyes!
'Puff!' quoth Hodge, thinking thereby to have fire without doubt;
With that Gib shut her two eyes and so the fire was out,
And by and by them opened even as they were before.
With that the sparks appeared even as they had done of yore;
And even as Hodge blew the fire, as he did think,
Gib, as she felt the blast, straightway began to wink,
Till Hodge fell of swearing, as came best to his turn,
The fire was sure bewitched and therefore would not burn.
At last Gib up the stairs, among the old posts and pins,
And Hodge, he hied him after till broke were both his shins,
Cursing and swearing oaths were never of his making,
That Gib would fire the house if that she were not taken!
... This is all the wit ye have when others make their moan!
Come down, Hodge! Where art thou? And let the cat alone!

amidst in the middle of
of yore before
fell of began
as ... turn such oaths as best served his purpose
were ... making that he certainly did not invent

An Ideal Husband

Oscar Wilde

This society comedy was first performed in 1895 at the Haymarket Theatre, London, and is set in fashionable London. SIR ROBERT CHILTERN is a highly respected politician and Under-Secretary for Foreign Affairs. Happily married to Lady Chiltern for several years, he is an 'ideal husband'. In this scene he confesses to his friend Lord Goring that he is being black-mailed by the unscrupulous Mrs Cheveley, who has a letter in her possession proving that, at the outset of his career, he sold a government secret in return for wealth, power and position.

Act 2

SIR ROBERT CHILTERN
[*Throws himself into an armchair by the writing-table*]
One night after dinner at Lord Radley's the Baron began talking about success in modern life as something that one could reduce to an absolutely definite science. With that wonderfully fascinating quiet voice of his he expounded to us the most terrible of all philosophies, the philosophy of power, preached to us the most marvellous of all gospels, the gospel of gold. I think he saw the effect he had produced on me, for some days afterwards he wrote and asked me to come and see him. He was living then in Park Lane, in the house Lord Woolcomb has now. I remember so well how, with a strange smile on his pale curved lips, he led me through his wonderful picture gallery, showed me his tapestries, his enamels, his jewels, his carved ivories, made me wonder at the strange loveliness of the luxury in which he lived; and then told me that luxury was nothing but a background, a painted scene in a play, and that power, power over other men, power over the world was the one thing worth having, the one supreme pleasure worth knowing, the one joy one never tired of, and that in our century only the rich possessed it . . . You have never been poor, and never known what ambition is. You cannot understand what a wonderful chance the Baron gave me. Such a chance as few men get . . . When I was going away he said to me that if I ever could give him any private information of real value he would make me a very rich man. I was dazed at the prospect he held out to me, and my ambition and my desire for power were at that time boundless. Six weeks later certain private documents passed through my hands . . . Weak? Oh, I am sick of hearing that phrase. Sick of using it about others. Weak? Do you really think, Arthur, that it is weakness that yields to temptation? I tell you that there are terrible temptations that it requires strength, strength and courage, to yield to. To stake all one's life on a single moment, to risk everything on one throw, whether the stake be power or pleasure, I care not – there is no weakness in that. There is a horrible, a terrible courage. I had that courage. I sat down that same afternoon and wrote Baron Arnheim the letter this woman now holds. He made three-quarters of a million over the transaction.

The Importance of Being Earnest

Oscar Wilde

This comedy of manners was first performed at the St James's
Theatre, London, in 1895. The opening scene is set in ALGERNON
MONCRIEFF's flat in Half Moon Street. ALGERNON is talking
to his friend, Jack Worthing, known to him at present as 'Ernest'.
He has found a cigarette case belonging to 'Ernest' and demands
to know why it is inscribed to 'dear Uncle Jack'. Jack confesses that
he has invented a younger brother called 'Ernest' in order to
escape up to town as much as possible. He is, in fact, 'Ernest' in
town and 'Jack' in the country. ALGERNON remarks that he is
obviously a 'Bunburyist' and goes on to explain the meaning of
the word.

   While they talk they eat up a whole plate of cucumber sand-
wiches and another of plain bread and butter, laid for
ALGERNON's Aunt Augusta and cousin Gwendolen's tea.

Act 1

ALGERNON

Literary criticism is not your forte dear fellow. Don't try it. You
should leave that to people who haven't been at a University. They
do it so well in the daily papers. What you really are is a Bunburyist.
I was quite right in saying you were a Bunburyist. You are one of the
most advanced Bunburyists I know ... You have invented a very
useful younger brother called Ernest, in order that you may be able
to come up to town as often as you like. I have invented an invaluable permanent invalid called Bunbury, in order that I may be able
to go down into the country whenever I choose. Bunbury is perfectly
invaluable. If it wasn't for Bunbury's extraordinary bad health, for
instance, I wouldn't be able to dine with you at Willis's to-night,
for I have been really engaged to Aunt Augusta for more than a
week ... To begin with, I dined there on Monday, and once a week
is quite enough to dine with one's own relations. In the second place,
whenever I do dine there I am always treated as a member of the
family, and sent down with either no woman at all, or two. In the
third place, I know perfectly well whom she will place me next to,
to-night. She will place me next Mary Farquhar, who always flirts
with her own husband across the dinner-table. That is not very
pleasant. Indeed, it is not even decent – and that sort of thing is
enormously on the increase. The amount of women in London who
flirt with their own husbands is perfectly scandalous. It looks so bad.
It is simply washing one's clean linen in public. Besides, now that I
know you to be a confirmed Bunburyist I naturally want to talk to
you about Bunburying. I want to tell you the rules ... Nothing will
induce me to part with Bunbury, and if you ever get married, which
seems to me extremely problematic, you will be very glad to know
Bunbury. A man who marries without knowing Bunbury has a very
tedious time of it.

The Knight of the Burning Pestle

Francis Beaumont

First performed sometime in 1610 or 1611 at the Blackfriars Theatre, London, and set in London, it is a play within a play and a satire of the merchant class with its taste for tales of knight-errants and damsels in distress. A grocer takes his wife to a play for the first time and they stop the action to insist that their apprentice, RAFE, takes part in it. RAFE becomes 'The Knight of the Burning Pestle' and involves himself in absurd and often uproarious adventures. In this scene, accompanied by his Squire and Dwarf he vows to rescue Mistress Merrythought and her son Michael – who, frightened by his strange appearance, are actually running away from him.

Act 2

RAFE
Lace on my helm again. What noise is this?
A gentle lady flying the embrace
Of some uncourteous knight? I will relieve her.
Go, squire, and say, the knight that wears this pestle
In honour of all ladies, swears revenge
Upon that recreant coward that pursues her.
Go comfort her, and that same gentle squire
That bears her company . . .

                                        [*Exit Tim*]

My trusty dwarf and friend, reach me my shield,
And hold it while I swear. First by my knighthood;
Then by the soul of Amadis de Gaul,
My famous ancestor, then by my sword
The beauteous Brionella girt about me;
By this bright burning pestle, of mine honour
The living trophy; and by all respect
Due to distressed damsels: here I vow
Never to end the quest of this fair lady
And that forsaken squire, till by my valour
I gain their liberty . . .
[*Enter Mistress Merrythought and Michael, and* [*Tim as*] *Squire*]
. . . Madam, if any service or devoir
Of a poor errant knight may right your wrongs,
Command it; I am prest to give you succour,
For to the holy end I bear my armour . . .
Young hope of valour, weep not; I am here
That will confound thy foe and pay it dear
Upon his coward head, that dares deny
Distressed squires and ladies equity.
I have but one horse, on which shall ride
This lady fair behind me, and before
This courteous squire; fortune will give us more
Upon our next adventure. Fairly speed
Beside us, squire and dwarf, to do us need.

devoir duty
prest prepared (French *prêt*)

79

Lady Windermere's Fan

Oscar Wilde

This society comedy or comedy of manners, was first performed at the St James's Theatre, London, in 1892 and is set in fashionable London. LORD WINDERMERE has been paying out large sums of money to the notorious divorcee, Mrs Erlynne, in return for her silence about the 'unfortunate' fact that she is his wife's mother. Lady Windermere, believing the rumours that her husband is infatuated with Mrs Erlynne, decides to run away with Lord Darlington who has declared his undying love for her. Mrs Erlynne, finding her daughter's farewell note, hurries to Darlington's rooms and persuades Lady Windermere to return home, but in doing so, compromises herself. In this scene she has called to return the fan that Lady Windermere left on Lord Darlington's sofa, saying that she herself had borrowed it and inadvertently left it there. Whilst Lady Windermere is out of the room, LORD WINDERMERE tells Mrs Erlynne that she has behaved disgracefully and has not told him the truth. To which she retorts, indicating Lady Windermere, 'I have not told *her* the truth, you mean'.

Act 4

LORD WINDERMERE

I sometimes wish you had. I should have been spared then the misery, the anxiety, the annoyance of the last six months. But rather than my wife should know – that the mother whom she was taught to consider as dead, the mother whom she has mourned as dead, is living – a divorced woman, going about under an assumed name, a bad woman preying upon life, as I know you now to be – rather than that, I was ready to supply you with money to pay bill after bill, extravagance after extravagance, to risk what occurred yesterday, the first quarrel I have ever had with my wife. You don't understand what that means to me. How could you? But I tell you that the only bitter words that ever came from those sweet lips of hers were on your account, and I hate to see you next her. You sully the innocence that is in her. And then I used to think that with all your faults you were frank and honest. You are not . . . You made me get you an invitation to my wife's ball . . . You came, and within an hour of your leaving the house you are found in a man's rooms – you are disgraced before everyone . . . Therefore I have a right to look upon you as what you are – a worthless, vicious woman. I have the right to tell you never to enter this house, never to attempt to come near my wife – . . . You have no right to claim her as your daughter. You left her, abandoned her when she was but a child in the cradle, abandoned her for your lover, who abandoned you in turn . . . Oh, I am not going to mince words for you. I know you thoroughly . . . For twenty years of your life you lived without your child, without a thought of your child. One day you read in the papers that she had married a rich man. You saw your hideous chance. You knew that to spare her the ignominy of learning that a woman like you was her mother, I would endure anything. You began your blackmailing . . . And as for your blunder in taking my wife's fan from here and then leaving it about in Darlington's rooms, it is unpardonable. I can't bear the sight of it now. I shall never let my wife use it again. The thing is soiled for me. You should have kept it and not brought it back.

Love for Love

William Congreve

This Restoration comedy was first performed in 1695 by His
Majesty's Servants at a theatre in Lincoln's Inn Fields, London,
and is set in London. BEN is a sailor and Sir Sampson's younger
son – described as 'a little rough' and in need of 'a little polish'.
He has just returned from a long sea voyage and his father is
anxious for him to marry and settle down. In this scene BEN
attempts to propose to Miss Prue, daughter of his father's friend,
old Foresight. However, she is already in love with Tattle and
wants nothing to do with him. (It is interesting to note that the
original BEN, played by Mr Dogget, was said to have taken up
lodgings in Wapping in order to perfect his sailor's part.)

Act 3, Scene 7

BEN

Come mistress, will you please to sit down, for an you stand astern a that'n, we shall never grapple together. Come, I'll haul a chair; there, an you please to sit, I'll sit by you ... Why, that's true, as you say, nor I an't dumb; I can be heard as far as another. I'll heave off to please you. [Sits farther off] An we were a league asunder, I'd undertake to hold discourse with you, an 'twere not a main high wind indeed, and full in my teeth. Look you forsooth, I am, as it were, bound for the land of matrimony; 'tis a voyage, d'ye see, that was none of my seeking. I was commanded by father, and if you like of it, mayhap I may steer into your harbour. How say you, mistress? The short of the thing is this, that if you like me, and I like you, we may chance to swing in a hammock together ... Now, for my part, d'ye see, I'm for carrying things above board, I'm not for keeping anything under hatches; so that if you ben't as willing as I, say so, a God's name, there's no harm done; mayhap you may be shamefaced; some maidens, tho'f they love a man well enough, yet they don't care to tell'n so to's face. If that's the case, why, silence gives consent ... Look you, young woman, you may learn to give good words, however. I spoke you fair, d'ye see, and civil. As for your love or your liking, I don't value it of a rope's end; and mayhap I like you as little as you do me: what I said was in obedience to father; gad, I fear a whipping no more than you do. But I tell you one thing, if you should give such language at sea, you'd have a cat-o'-nine-tails laid cross your shoulders. Flesh! who are you? You heard t'other handsome young woman speak civilly to me of her own accord. Whatever you think of yourself, gad, I don't think you are any more to compare to her, than a can of small beer to a bowl of punch ... What does father mean to leave me alone as soon as I come home with such a dirty dowdy? Sea-calf? I an't calf enough to lick your chalked face, you cheese-curd you. Marry thee! Ouns, I'll marry a Lapland witch as soon, and live upon selling of contrary winds and wrecked vessels.

astern a that'n she has turned her back on him

The Malcontent

John Marston

This tragi-comedy seems to have been written sometime between 1600 and 1604 for the Children of the Queen's Revels and then acquired by the King's Men and presented, with additional material, at the Globe Theatre in London.

The central figure is the deposed Duke of Genoa, Giovanni Altofronto, who in his disguise as the malcontent, Malevole, manages to remain an active force in the society from which he has been excluded, commentating throughout with detached cynicism on the hypocrisy and corruption of the Court. The villain of the piece is MENDOZA, described as a 'minion to the Duchess of Pietro Iacomo', who, having successfully plotted the downfall of Altofronto, rejoices in his role as the new Duke's favourite.

In this scene, MENDOZA is exulting over his great good fortune and at the same time boasting of having cuckolded the Duke by seducing his Duchess, the 'beauteous' Aurelia.

Act 1, Scene 5

MENDOZA

Now, good Elysium, what a delicious heaven is it for a man to be in a prince's favour! O sweet God! O pleasure! O fortune! O all thou best of life! What should I think, what say, what do? To be a favourite, a minion! To have a general timorous respect observe a man, a stateful silence in his presence, solitariness in his absence, a confused hum and busy murmur of obsequious suitors training him; the cloth held up, and way proclaimed before him; petitionary vassals licking the pavement with their slavish knees, whilst some odd palace-lamprels that engender with snakes, and are full of eyes on both sides, with a kind of insinuated humbleness fix all their delights upon his brow. O blessed state, what a ravishing prospect doth the Olympus of favour yield! Death, I cornute the duke! Sweet women, most sweet ladies – nay, angels! By heaven, he is more accursed than a devil that hates you, or is hated by you; and happier than a god that loves you, or is beloved by you. You preservers of mankind, life-blood of society, who would live – nay, who can live without you? O paradise, how majestical is your austerer presence! How imperiously chaste is your more modest face! But, O, how full of ravishing attraction is your pretty, petulant, languishing, lasciviously-composed countenance! These amorous smiles, those soul-warming sparkling glances, ardent as those flames that singed the world by heedless Phacton. In body how delicate, in soul how witty, in discourse how pregnant, in life how wary, in favours how judicious, in day how sociable, and in night how – O pleasure unutterable! Indeed, it is most certain, one man cannot deserve only to enjoy a beauteous woman. But a duchess? In despite of Phoebus I'll write a sonnet instantly in praise of her.

[*Exit*]

observe defer to
stateful dignified
training following in his train
lamprels young lampreys
cornute make cuckold

A New Way to Pay Old Debts

Philip Massinger

First performed in 1625 by the Queen's Men, possibly at the Phoenix, Drury Lane, London, and set in the country near Nottingham. At the opening of the play, TIMOTHY TAPWELL – an ale-house keeper – and his wife Froth, on orders from the sinister Sir Giles Overreach, have refused to serve either drink or tobacco to Sir Giles' nephew, Welborne, a young gentleman forced into heavy debt with little hope of recovery. In this scene Wellborn, has found a way to pay off his creditors and is accepted back into society. He appears once more to be 'his uncle's darling' and TAPWELL fears that Wellborn will expose them for receiving stolen goods and keeping a bawdy house.

Act 4, Scene 2

TAPWELL
Undone, undone! This was your counsel, Froth.
       ... now he's his uncle's darling, and has got
Master Justice Greedy (since he fill'd his belly)
At his commandment, to do anything;
Woe, woe to us ...
Troth, we do not deserve it at his hands:
Though he knew all the passages of our house;
As the receiving of stol'n goods, and bawdry,
When he was rogue Welborne, no man would believe him,
And then his information could not hurt us.
But now he is right worshipful again,
Who dares but doubt his testimony? Me thinks
I see thee Froth already in a cart
For a close bawd, thine eyes ev'n pelted out
With dirt, and rotten eggs, and my hand hissing
(If I scape the halter) with the letter R,
Printed upon it ...
He has summon'd all his creditors by the drum,
And they swarm about him like so many soldiers
On the pay day, and has found out such a new way
To pay his old debts, as 'tis very likely
He shall be chronicl'd for it.

passages goings-on
close secret

The Plain Dealer

William Wycherley

First performed in 1676 at the Theatre Royal, London, this Restoration comedy attacks the double-dealing of Wycherley's society, the perversion of justice, the hypocrisy and malicious gossip. The action revolves around CAPTAIN MANLY, the 'plain dealer' of the title, who is described as 'honest, surly and having chosen a life at sea in order to avoid the world'. He is in love with Olivia, who pretends to hate the 'lying, masking world' as much as he does, but at heart is affected, prudish and deceitful. MANLY has just completed his latest voyage and is expecting Olivia to be eagerly awaiting his return.

In this scene he arrives at her lodging, accompanied by his Lieutenant, Freeman, and happens to overhear her gossiping with her friends, Master Novel and Lord Plausible. As usual they are tearing reputations to shreds and MANLY himself is the target of their vicious attack. All three are deriding the 'silly rogues' who are 'ambitious of losing their arms' and 'come home looking like a pair of compasses'. When Olivia comments that she hates a 'lover that smells of Thames Street', MANLY can bear it no longer and steps forward to confront them all.

Act 2, Scene 1

MANLY

[*Aside*] I can bear no longer, and need her no more. [*To Olivia*] But since you have these two pulvilio boxes, these essence bottles, this pair of musk-cats here, I hope I may venture to come yet nearer you ... You have fitted me for believing you could not be fickle though you were young, could not dissemble love though 'twas your interest, nor be vain though you were handsome, nor break your promise though to a parting lover, nor abuse your best friend though you had wit; but I take not your contempt of me worse than your esteem or civility for these things here, though you know 'em ... Yes, things! [*Coming up to Novel*] Canst thou be angry, thou thing? ... Thy courage will appear more by thy belt than thy sword, I dare swear. – Then, madam, [*Indicating Plausible*] for this gentle piece of courtesy, this man of tame honour, what could you find in him? Was it his languishing, affected tone, his mannerly look, his second-hand flattery, the refuse of the playhouse tiring-rooms? Or his slavish obsequiousness, in watching at the door of your box at the playhouse for your hand to your chair? Or his janty way of playing with your fan? Or was it the gunpowder spot on his hand, or the jewel in his ear, that purchased your heart? ... [*To Novel and Lord Plausible*] Why, you impudent, pitiful wretches, you presume, sure, upon your effeminacy to urge me, for you are in all things so like women that you may think it in me a kind of cowardice to beat you ... Or perhaps you think this lady's presence secures you. But have a care; she has talked herself out of all the respect I had for her, and by using me ill before you has given me a privilege of using you so before her. But if you would preserve your respect to her, and not be beaten before her, go, be gone immediately ... Be gone, I say. Your suburb mistresses beyond the Tower part with their lovers, just as you did from me, with unforced vows of constancy and floods of willing tears, but the same winds bear away their lovers and their vows; and for their grief, if the credulous, unexpected fools return, they find new comforters, fresh cullies, such as I found here. The mercenary love of those women too suffers shipwreck with their gallants' fortunes; now you have heard chance has used me scurvily, therefore you do too. Well, persevere in your ingratitude, falsehood, and disdain; have constancy in something, and I promise you to be as just to your real scorn as I was to your feigned love, and henceforward will despise, contemn, hate, loathe, and detest you, most faithfully.

bear intransitive

pulvilio perfumed powder for dressing wigs

musk-cats animals secreting musk, the basis of many perfumes

tiring-rooms dressing-rooms

hand to your chair Plausible escorts Olivia to her sedan after the play.

janty well-bred, genteel, elegant

gunpowder spot a blue beauty spot tattooed into the skin with gunpowder

The Provoked Wife

John Vanbrugh

First performed at the New Theatre in Lincoln's Inn Fields,
London, in 1697, this Restoration comedy is set in fashionable
London and revolves around the unsuitable marriage of SIR
JOHN and Lady Brute and their separate efforts to reach some
sort of compromise. SIR JOHN, coming home one night in a
drunken stupor, discovers two young men, Constant and
Heartfree, hiding in his wife's closet, and accuses her of cuck-
olding him. Next morning Constant calls to explain matters, but
SIR JOHN refuses to listen. However, when Constant suggests
that it might be better to settle by the sword SIR JOHN says he
needs time to think things over.

Act 5, Scene 5

SIR JOHN

Lord, sir, you are very hasty! If I had been found at prayers in your
wife's closet, I should have allowed you twice as much time to come
to yourself in ... [*Aside*] 'Tis well – 'tis very well! In spite of that
young jade's matrimonial intrigue, I am a downright stinking cuckold. – [*Putting his hand to his forehead*] Here they are. Boo! Methinks
I could butt with a bull. – What the plague did I marry her for? I
knew she did not like me; if she had, she would have lain with me,
for I would have done so because I liked her. But that's past, and I
have her. – And now, what shall I do with her? If I put my horns in
my pocket, she'll grow insolent. If I don't, that goat there, that stal-
lion, is ready to whip me through the guts. The debate then is
reduced to this: shall I die a hero or live a rascal? – Why, wiser men
than I have long since concluded that a living dog is better than a
dead lion. – [*To Constant and Heartfree*] Gentlemen, now my wine and
my passion are governable, I must own I have never observed anything in my wife's course of life to back me in my jealousy of her.
But jealousy's a mark of love; so she need not trouble her head about
it, as long as I make no more words on't ... Your humble servant. –
[*Aside*] A wheedling son of a whore!

The Provoked Wife

John Vanbrugh

First performed at the New Theatre in Lincoln's Inn Fields, London, in 1697, this Restoration comedy is set in fashionable London and revolves around the unsuitable marriage of Sir John and Lady Brute and their separate efforts to reach some sort of compromise. For almost two years Constant has been courting Lady Brute, although she has never given him the slightest encouragement. In this scene he pours out his soul to his friend, HEARTFREE, who never has any problems with his romantic encounters and has no time at all for love. Constant remarks that the only thing that can possibly relieve his misery is if HEARTFREE himself should fall in love. HEARTFREE assures him that this will never happen.

Act 2, Scene 1

HEARTFREE

That day will never come, be assured, Ned. Not but that I can pass a night with a woman, and for the time, perhaps, make myself as good sport as you can do. Nay, I can court a woman too, call her nymph, angel, goddess – what you please. But here's the difference 'twixt you and I: I persuade a woman she's an angel; she persuades you she's one. – Prithee, let me tell you how I avoid falling in love; that which serves me for prevention, may chance to serve you for a cure . . . I always consider a woman, not as the tailor, the shoemaker, the tire-woman, the sempstress, and (which is more than all that) the poet makes her; but I consider her as pure nature has contrived her, and that more strictly than I should have done our old grandmother Eve, had I seen her naked in the garden; for I consider her turned inside out. Her heart well examined, I find there pride, vanity, covet-ousness, indiscretion, but above all things – malice: plots eternally a-forging to destroy one another's reputations, and as honestly to charge the levity of men's tongues with the scandal; hourly debates how to make poor gentlemen in love with 'em, with no other intent but to use 'em like dogs when they have done; a constant desire of doing more mischief, and an everlasting war waged against truth and good nature . . . Then for her outside, I consider it merely as an outside; she has a thin tiffany covering over just such stuff as you and I are made on. As for her motion, her mien, her airs, and all those tricks, I know they affect you mightily. If you should see your mistress at a coronation, dragging her peacock's train with all her state and insolence about her, 'twould strike you with all the awful thoughts that heaven itself could pretend to from you; whereas I turn the whole matter into a jest, and suppose her strutting in the self-same stately manner, with nothing on but her stays and her under scanty quilted petticoat.

tire-woman dressmaker
tiffany a kind of transparent silk
under . . . petticoat a short padded underskirt of coarse cloth

The Relapse

John Vanbrugh

This Restoration comedy was first performed in 1696 at the
Theatre Royal, Drury Lane, London. The action revolves around
the reconciliation of the virtuous Amanda and her profligate
husband, LOVELESS, who after begging forgiveness and
swearing undying love, immediately falls for his wife's cousin,
the beautiful Berinthia. Earlier in the play, LOVELESS confesses
to Amanda that he was very much attracted by a young lady at
the theatre the previous night but, of course, being a reformed
character he was easily able to put any licentious thoughts out
of his mind. To his astonishment the young lady turns out to be
his wife's cousin, and to make matters worse, Amanda invites
her to stay with them. In this soliloquy he acknowledges how
much he owes to his wife and, at the same time, tries to ra-
tionalise his surge of feeling for Berinthia.

Act 3, Scene 2

LOVELESS
Is my wife within? . . .
'Tis well, leave me.

[*Exit Servant*]

Sure Fate has yet some business to be done,
Before Amanda's heart and mine must rest;
Else, why amongst those legions of her sex,
Which throng the world,
Should she pick out for her companion
The only one on earth
Whom nature has endow'd for her undoing?
Undoing, was't I said – who shall undo her?
Is not her empire fix'd? am I not hers?

94

Did she not rescue me, a grovelling slave,
When chained and bound by that black tyrant vice,
I laboured in his vilest drudgery?
Did she not ransom me, and set me free?
Nay, more: when by my follies sunk
To a poor, tattered, despicable beggar,
Did she not lift me up to envied fortune?
Give me herself, and all that she possessed,
Without a thought of more return,
Than what a poor repenting heart might make her?
Han't she done this? And if she has,
Am I not strongly bound to love her for it?
To love her! – Why, do I not love her then?
By Earth and Heaven I do!
Nay, I have demonstration that I do:
For I would sacrifice my life to serve her.
Yet hold – if laying down my life
Be demonstration of my love,
What is't I feel in favour of Berinthia?

For should she be in danger, methinks I could incline to risk it for
her service too; and yet I do not love her. How then subsists my
proof? – Oh, I have found it out! What I would do for one, is demonstration of my love; and if I'd do as much for t'other, it there is
demonstration of my friendship. Ay, it must be so. I find I'm very
much her friend. – Yet let me ask myself one puzzling question more.
Whence springs this might friendship all at once? For our acquaintance is of later date. Now friendship's said to be a plant of tedious
growth; its root composed of tender fibres, nice in their taste, cau-
tious in spreading, checked with the last corruption in the soil; long
ere it take, and longer still ere it appear to do so: whilst mine is in a
moment shot so high, and fix'd so fast, it seems beyond the power
of storms to shake it. I doubt it thrives too fast.

[*Musing*]
[*Enter Berinthia*]

Ha! she here! – Nay, then take heed, my heart, for there are dangers
towards.

it there is if there is

The Revenger's Tragedy

Anon

The authorship of this play is uncertain. It was registered in the
Stationers' Registry in 1607, performed by His Majesty's Servants
and is possibly an episode in the history of the Medici family.
VINDICE – the name means 'a revenger of wrongs' – has sworn
to avenge his beloved Gloriana, who was poisoned by the Duke
because she would not 'consent unto his palsey-lust'. Assisted
by his brother, Hippolito, he devises ingenious deaths for the
Duke and his family. In this scene, he tells Hippolito that he has
procured a 'woman' for the Duke to satisfy his lust and to be
enjoyed secretly. The 'woman' is the skull of the dead Gloriana,
decked out in her finery – her lips painted with flesh eating
poison.

Act 3, Scene 5

VINDICE
Does every proud and self-affecting dame
Camphor her face for this, and grieve her maker
In sinful baths of milk, when many an infant starves
For her superfluous outside – all for this?
Who now bids twenty pound a night, prepares
Music, perfumes and sweetmeats? All are hushed,
Thou may'st lie chaste now! It were fine methinks
To have thee seen at revels, forgetful feasts
And unclean brothels; sure 'twould fright the sinner
And make him a good coward, put a reveller
Out of his antic amble
And cloy an epicure with empty dishes.
Here might a scornful and ambitious woman
Look through and through herself; see, ladies, with false forms
You deceive men but cannot deceive worms.
Now to my tragic business. Look you brother,
I have not fashioned this only for show
And useless property, no – it shall bear a part
E'en in it own revenge. This very skull,
Whose mistress the duke poisoned with this drug,
The mortal curse of the earth, shall be revenged
In the like strain and kiss his lips to death.
As much as the dumb thing can, he shall feel;
What fails in poison we'll supply in steel.

Camphor aromatic base for cosmetics
superfluous outside excessively pampered appearance or exterior
property i.e. theatrical stage accessory

The Rivals

Richard Brinsley Sheridan

This eighteenth-century comedy of manners was first performed at the Theatre Royal, Covent Garden, London, in 1775. Set in Bath, it revolves around the rivals for the hand of the lovely Lydia Languish and the subsequent intrigues leading up to a comic attempt at a duel, arranged by SIR LUCIUS O'TRIGGER – a penniless Irish baronet. Meanwhile, Lydia's middle-aged Aunt, Mrs Malaprop, has developed a passion for SIR LUCIUS and is sending him love letters via her unscrupulous maid, Lucy, who has persuaded the baronet that he is corresponding not with the Aunt, but with Lydia.

In this scene, Lucy brings SIR LUCIUS the latest letter from his 'dear Dalia', making sure that she receives her usual reward.

Act 2, Scene 2

SIR LUCIUS

Hah! my little embassadress – upon my conscience I have been look-ing for you; I have been on the South Parade this half-hour ... The North Parade! Faith! – maybe that was the reason we did not meet; and it is very comical too, how you could go out and I not see you – for I was only taking a nap at the Parade coffee-house, and I chose the window on purpose that I might not miss you ... Sure enough it must have been so – and I never dreamt it was so late, till I waked. Well, but my little girl, have you got nothing for me? ... O faith! I guessed you weren't come empty-handed – well – let me see what the dear creature says ... [*Lucy gives him a letter, reads*] *Sir – there is often a sudden incentive impulse in love, that has a greater induc-tion than years of domestic combination: such was the commotion I felt at the first superfluous view of Sir Lucius O'Trigger.* Very pretty, upon my word. *Female punctuation forbids me to say more; yet let me add, that it*

98

will give me joy infallible to find Sir Lucius worthy the last criterion of my affections. – Delia. Upon my conscience! Lucy, your lady is a great mistress of language. Faith, she's quite the queen of the dictionary! – for the devil a word dare refuse coming at her call – though one would think it was quite out of hearing . . . Faith, she must be very deep read to write this way – though she is a rather arbitrary writer too – for here are a great many poor words pressed into the service of this note, that would get their *habeas corpus* from any court in Christendom. – However, when affection guides the pen, Lucy, he must be a brute who finds fault with the style . . . tell her, I'll make her the best husband in the world, and Lady O'Trigger into the bargain! But we must get the old gentlewoman's consent – and do everything fairly . . . I am so poor that I can't afford to do a dirty action. If I did not want money I'd steal your mistress and her fortune with a great deal of pleasure. – However, my pretty girl, [*Gives her money*] here's a little something to buy you a riband; and meet me in the evening, and I'll give you an answer to this. So, hussy, take a kiss beforehand, to put you in mind.

incentive provocative, arousing
induction in a strained sense, an introductory process; or for, inducement
commotion for, emotion?
superfluous for, superficial
punctuation for, punctilio
infallible possibly in the sense of 'certain'; or for, ineffable
pressed forcibly enlisted, as by the press-gang
habeas corpus release (from the opening words of a writ which prevents a person being imprisoned without charge)

The Rover

Aphra Behn

First performed in 1677 at the Duke's Theatre, London, this Restoration comedy is set in the 1650s in Naples during carnival time. In England, Cromwell's Protectorate had suppressed such 'bawdy' activities, but abroad a young Englishman was free to enjoy himself in a way he could never hope to at home.

The action centres around Willmore – the Rover – who steps ashore in search of 'love and mirth' and is greeted by his friends from England. He is introduced to BLUNT, a young country gentleman, described as a wealthy 'Essex calf' who cheerfully helps fund their amorous adventures. BLUNT, despite his companion's warnings, is lured to the courtesan Lucetta's house. There he is duped and robbed, divested of his clothing and ends up in a 'common sewer'.

In this scene we see him climbing out of the sewer, his face dirty, and in his underwear.

Act 3, Scene 4

BLUNT [*climbing up*]

Oh Lord! I am got out at last and, which is a miracle, without a clue. And now to damning and cursing! But if that would ease me, where shall I begin? With my fortune, myself, or the quean that cozened me? What a dog was I to believe in Woman? Oh, coxcomb! Ignorant, conceited coxcomb! To fancy she could be enamoured with my person! At first sight, enamoured! Oh, I'm a cursed puppy! 'Tis plain, 'Fool' was writ upon my forehead! She perceived it – saw the Essex calf there. For what allurements could there be in this countenance, which I can endure because I'm acquainted with it? Oh, dull, silly dog! To be thus soothed into a cozening! Had I been drunk, I might fondly have credited the young quean! But as I was in my right wits, to be thus cheated confirms it I am a dull, believing, English country fop. – But my comrades! Death and the devil, there's the worst of all! Then a ballad will be sung tomorrow on the Prado, to a lousy tune of the Enchanted Squire and the Annihilated Damsel. – But Fred, that rogue, and the colonel will abuse me beyond all Christian patience! Had she left me my clothes, I have a bill of exchange at home would've saved my credit – but now all hope is taken from me. Well, I'll home – if I can find the way – with this consolation, that I am not the first kind, believing coxcomb, but there are, gallants, many such good natures amongst ye.

And though you've better arts to hide your follies,
'Adsheartlikins, y'are all as arrant cullies.

---

quean hussy

Prado a fashionable promenade; i.e. a popular public place

The School for Scandal

Richard Brinsley Sheridan

This comedy of manners was first performed at Drury Lane, London, in 1777 and is set in fashionable London. At the centre of the play is the group of scandal mongers – 'The School' – who meet on a regular basis to tear the reputations of their friends and relatives to pieces. CHARLES SURFACE, an extravagant but good hearted young man, is in love with Sir Peter Teazle's ward, Maria. But the scandal mongers have so damaged his reputation, urged on by his mealy mouthed brother, Joseph, that Sir Peter wants nothing to do with him. His Uncle, Sir Oliver Surface, has just returned from the Far East and is about to decide which of his two nephews shall be his heir. He tells Sir Peter that he is determined not to be influenced in his choice by malicious gossip but will make a 'trial of their hearts'. Aided by Moses, a money lender, he disguises himself as a 'Mr Premium', a gentleman from the City who is prepared to advance money.

In this scene, CHARLES welcomes 'Mr Premium' and takes him to The Picture Room, where he proceeds to auction the paintings of his forefathers.

Act 4, Scene 1

CHARLES
Walk in, gentlemen, pray walk in. Here they are, the family of the Surfaces, up to the Conquest ... these are done in the true spirit of portrait painting – no *volontière grace* and expression, not like the works of your modern Raphael, who gives you the strongest resemblance, yet contrives to make your own portrait independent of you, so that you may sink the original and not hurt the picture. No, no; the merit of these is the inveterate likeness – all stiff and awkward as the originals, and like nothing in human nature beside ... You see,

102

Master Premium, what a domestic character I am. Here I sit of an evening surrounded by my family. But come, get to your pulpit, Mr Auctioneer. Here's an old gouty chair of my grandfather's will answer the purpose ... [*Reading a roll*] What parchment have we here? *Richard, heir to Thomas.* Oh, our genealogy in full. Here, Careless, you shall have no common bit of mahogany – here's the family tree for you, you rogue. This shall be your hammer, and now you may knock down my ancestors with their own pedigree ... Well, here's my great-uncle Sir Richard Raveline, a marvellous good general in his day, I assure you. He served in all the Duke of Marlborough's wars, and got that cut over his eye at the Battle of Malplaquet. What say you, Mr Premium? Look at him – there's a hero for you! Not cut out of his feathers, as your modern clipped captains are, but enveloped in wig and regimentals, as a general should be. What do you bid? Careless, knock down my uncle Richard. Here now is a maiden sister of his, my great-aunt Deborah, done by Kneller, thought to be in his best manner, and a very formidable likeness. There she is, you see, a shepherdess feeding her flock. You shall have her for five pounds ten – the sheep are worth the money ... Knock down my aunt Deborah. Here now are two that were a sort of cousins of theirs. You see, Moses, these pictures were done some time ago, when beaux wore wigs, and the ladies their own hair ... This now is a grandfather of my mother's, a learned judge, well known on the western circuit. What do you rate him at, Moses? ... Four guineas! Gad's life, you don't bid me the price of his wig. Mr Premium, you have more respect for the woolsack. Do let us knock his lordship down at fifteen ... And these are two brothers of his, William and Walter Blunt, Esquires, both Members of Parliament and noted speakers; and what's very extraordinary, I believe this is the first time they were ever bought and sold ... Here's a jolly fellow. I don't know what relation, but he was Mayor of Manchester. Take him at eight pounds ... Come, make it guineas, and I'll throw you the two aldermen there into the bargain ... Careless, knock down the Lord Mayor and aldermen. But, plague on't, we shall be all day retailing in this manner. Do let us deal wholesale, what say you, little Premium? Give us three hundred pounds for the rest of the family in the lump ... What, that? Oh, that's my uncle Oliver. 'Twas done before he went to India ... No hang it! I'll not part with poor Noll. The old fellow has been very good to me, and egad I'll keep his picture while I've a room to put it in.

She Stoops to Conquer

Oliver Goldsmith

This eighteenth-century comedy was first produced at the Theatre Royal, Covent Garden, London, in 1773. It is set in HARDCASTLE's country mansion and parodies the sentimental comedies popular at that time. HARDCASTLE and his friend, Sir Charles Marlow have arranged a match between HARDCASTLE's daughter, Kate and Young Marlow. In this scene Young Marlow and his friend Hastings are expected down from London and HARDCASTLE is training his 'four awkward servants' to wait at table.

Act 2, Scene 1

HARDCASTLE

Well, I hope you're perfect in the table exercise I have been teaching you these three days. You all know your posts and your places, and can show that you have been used to good company, without ever stirring from home ... When company comes, you are not to pop out and stare, and then run in again, like frighted rabbits in a warren ... You, Diggory, whom I have taken from the barn, are to make a show at the side-table; and you, Roger, whom I have advanced from the plough, are to place yourself behind *my* chair. But you're not to stand so, with your hands in your pockets. Take your hands from your pockets, Roger; and from your head, you blockhead you. See how Diggory carries his hands. They're a little too stiff, indeed, but that's no great matter ... You must not be so talkative, Diggory. You must be all attention to the guests. You must hear us talk, and not think of talking; you must see us drink, and not think of drinking; you must see us eat, and not think of eating ... Blockhead! Is not a belly-full in the kitchen as good as a belly-full in the parlour? Stay your stomach with that reflection ... Diggory, you are too talkative. Then if I happen to say a good thing, or tell a good story at table, you must not all burst out a-laughing, as if you made part of the company ... Old Grouse in the gun-room! Ha! ha! ha! The story is a good one. Well, honest Diggory, you may laugh at that – but still remember to be attentive. Suppose one of the company should call for a glass of wine, how will you behave? A glass of wine, sir, if you please – [*To Diggory*] Eh, why don't you move? What, will nobody move? ... You numbskulls! and so while, like your betters, you are quarrelling for places, the guests must be starved. Oh you dunces! I find I must begin all over again. – But don't I hear a coach drive into the yard? To your posts, you blockheads. I'll go in the meantime and give my old friend's son a hearty reception at the gate.

Grouse a common name for a dog; no connotation yet of 'grumble'

places a pun: 'place' could mean simply 'position', as now, or 'government appointment' (1558)

She Stoops to Conquer

Oliver Goldsmith

This eighteenth-century comedy was first produced at the Theatre Royal, Covent Garden, London, in 1773. It is set in the Hardcastle's country mansion and parodies the sentimental comedies popular at that time. The action revolves around the arranged match and courtship between the Hardcastle's daughter Kate and Young Marlow, and the practical jokes played on family and friends by TONY LUMPKIN, Mrs Hardcastle's son by a former marriage. TONY has been ordered by his mother to marry his cousin, Constance, but he wants nothing to do with her. When he discovers she is in love with Marlow's friend, Hastings, he is only too delighted to help the lovers elope together. His mother discovers the plot and insists on accompanying Constance to her Aunt Pedigree's home, thirty miles away. TONY takes charge of the coach journey, driving them round and round the neighbouring countryside, finally tipping everyone into the local duck pond. Here he describes the adventure to Hastings, whose only concern is for Constance's safety.

Act 5, Scene 2

TONY

Ay, I'm your friend, and the best friend you have in the world, if you knew but all. This riding by night, by the bye, is cursedly tiresome. It has shook me worse than the basket of a stage-coach . . . Five and twenty miles in two hours and a half is no such bad driving. The poor beasts have smoked for it: rabbit me, but I'd rather ride forty miles after a fox, than ten with such varment . . . Left them? Why where should I leave them, but where I found them? . . . Riddle me this then. What's that goes round the house, and round the house, and never touches the house? . . . Why that's it, mon. I have led them astray. By jingo, there's not a pond or slough within five miles of the place but they can tell the taste of . . . You shall hear. I first took them down Feather-bed Lane, where we stuck fast in the mud. I then rattled them crack over the stones of Up-and-down Hill – I then introduced them to the gibbet on Heavy-tree Heath, and from that, with a circumbendibus, I fairly lodged them in the horse-pond at the bottom of the garden . . . No, no. Only mother is confoundedly frightened. She thinks herself forty miles off. She's sick of the journey, and the cattle can scarce crawl. So if your own horses be ready, you may whip off with cousin, and I'll be bound that no soul here can budge a foot to follow you . . . Ay, now it's dear friend, noble Squire. Just now, it was all idiot, cub, and run me through the guts. Damn *your* way of fighting, I say. After we take a knock in this part of the country, we kiss and be friends. But if you had run me through the guts, then I should be dead, and you might go kiss the hangman . . . Never fear me. Here she comes. Vanish. She's got from the pond, and draggled up to the waist like a mermaid. [*Enter Mrs Hardcastle*] Alack, mama, it was all your own fault. You would be for running away by night, without knowing one inch of the way.

smoked galloped at speed
rabbit me like 'drat me', a meaningless oath
varment vermin; hence, objectionable people (first usage)
circumbendibus roundabout process
cattle stable slang for 'horses'
draggled dirtied by being dragged through wet mud

The Shoemaker's Holiday

Thomas Dekker

This London comedy was most probably first performed at the Rose Theatre, London, in the late summer or autumn of 1599. It tells the story of a shoemaker, SIMON EYRE, who through his hard work and popularity amongst his workers and their families, rises to become Lord Mayor of London.

At the beginning of this scene EYRE is preparing for his Mayoral Banquet, and talking to Roland Lacy, who disguised as 'Hans' – a Dutch shoemaker – is about to marry his sweetheart, Rose. EYRE sends his wife Margery off to witness the ceremony, promising everyone a share of the feast on their return. Meanwhile, he makes ready to receive the King.

Scene 17

EYRE

This is the morning then – stay, my bully, my honest Hans: is it not? ... Away with these ifs and ans, Hans, and these etceteras. By mine honour, Roland Lacy, none but the King shall wrong thee. Come, fear nothing. Am not I Sim Eyre? Is not Sim Eyre Lord Mayor of London? ... Why, my sweet Lady Madgy, think you Simon Eyre can forget his fine Dutch journeyman? No, vah! Fie, I scorn it. It shall never be cast in my teeth that I was unthankful. Lady Madgy, thou hadst never covered thy Saracen's head with this French flap, nor loaden thy bum with this farthingale – 'tis trash, trumpery, vanity! – Simon Eyre had never walked in a red petticoat, nor wore a chain of gold, but for my fine journeyman's portagues; and shall I leave him? No. Prince am I none, yet bear a princely mind ... Lady Madgy, Lady Madgy, take two or three of my piecrust eaters, my buff-jerkin varlets, that do walk in black gowns at Simon Eyre's heels. Take them, good Lady Madgy, trip and go, my brown Queen of Periwigs, with my delicate

Rose and my jolly Roland to the Savoy, see them linked, countenance the marriage, and when it is done, cling, cling together, you Hamborow turtle-doves. I'll bear you out. Come to Simon Eyre, come dwell with me, Hans, thou shalt eat minced pies and marchpane. Rose, away, cricket. Trip and go, my Lady Madgy, to the Savoy! Hans, wed and to bed; kiss and away – go, vanish . . . [*Margery, Lacy and Rose go out*] Go, vanish, vanish; avaunt, I say. By the Lord of Ludgate, it's a mad life to be a Lord Mayor. It's a stirring life, a fine life, a velvet life, a careful life. Well, Simon Eyre, yet set a good face on it, in the honour of Saint Hugh. Soft, the King this day comes to dine with me, to see my new buildings. His Majesty is welcome; he shall have good cheer, delicate cheer, princely cheer. This day my fellow prentices of London come to dine with me too. They shall have fine cheer, gentlemanlike cheer. I promised the mad Cappadocians, when we all served at the conduit together, that if ever I came to be Mayor of London, I would feast them all; and I'll do't, I'll do't, by the life of Pharaoh, by this beard, Sim Eyre will be no flincher. Besides, I have procured that upon every Shrove Tuesday, at the sound of the pancake bell, my fine dapper Assyrian lads shall clap up their shop windows and away. This is the day, and this day they shall do't, they shall do't!
Boys, that day are you free; let masters care,
And prentices shall pray for Simon Eyre.

stay Eyre has to restrain Lacy's eagerness
bully mate, comrade
Saracen's head referring to the ugly caricature on an inn-sign
red petticoat the Lord Mayor's scarlet gown
portagues Portuguese gold coins worth about £5, a considerable sum then
buff-jerkin varlets Eyre's irreverent term for the officers now under his command
brown lusty
countenance witness
Hamborow Hamburg
marchpane marzipan (i.e. you'll live in luxury)
velvet . . . careful Both terms convey Eyre's awareness of the cares and duties of rank; 'velvet-jacket' was slang for a mayor.
served . . . together i.e. as apprentices, fetching water for their masters' houses
pancake bell the bell for Church on Shrove Tuesday, but with obvious festive associations. The day was a traditional apprentices' holiday.
windows wooden shutters which let down to form shop counters.

The Spanish Tragedy

Thomas Kyd

Written sometime between 1582 and 1592 and performed by Lord Strange's Men for theatrical entrepreneur Philip Henslowe in 1592, it is one of the earlier Elizabethan revenge tragedies.

Overseeing the main action is the ghost of Don Andrea, who is seeking revenge for his death in battle at the hands of DON BALTHAZAR, Prince of Portingale*. He is accompanied by the personification of 'Revenge', who promises him vengeance and the opportunity to watch the tortuous route by which his enemy reaches his inevitable destruction.

Early in the play, BALTHAZAR is captured in battle, but his life is spared by the King of Spain and he is put into the charge of two captors, Lorenzo and Horatio, who treat him with great courtesy and friendship. He falls in love with the desirable Bel-Imperia, daughter of the Duke of Castile and Andrea's former beloved, but discovers she is being wooed by Horatio.

In this scene he conspires with Lorenzo to be revenged on Horatio. Lorenzo has already sent Bel-Imperia's servant to find out where the lovers plan to meet and asks BALTHAZAR how he likes 'this stratagem'.

* Portugal

Act 2, Scene 2

BALTHAZAR
Both well, and ill: it makes me glad and sad:
Glad, that I know the hinderer of my love,
Sad, that I fear she hates me whom I love.
Glad, that I know on whom to be revenged,
Sad, that she'll fly me if I take revenge.
Yet must I take revenge or die myself,
For love resisted grows impatient.
I think Horatio be my destined plague:
First, in his hand he brandished a sword,
And with that sword he fiercely waged war,
And in that war he gave me dangerous wounds,
And by those wounds he forced me to yield,
And by my yielding I became his slave.
Now in his mouth he carries pleasing words,
Which pleasing words do harbour sweet conceits,
Which sweet conceits are limed with sly deceits,
Which sly deceits smooth Bel-Imperia's ears,
And through her ears dive down into her heart,
And in her heart set him where I should stand.
Thus hath he ta'en my body by his force,
And now by sleight would captivate my soul:
But in his fall I'll tempt the destinies,
And either lose my life, or win my love.

sweet conceits pleasing figures of speech
limed with made into traps with (from bird-lime, a gluey substance used to catch birds)
smooth seduce, flatter
sleight trickery
in his fall in causing his downfall

The Spanish Tragedy

Thomas Kyd

Written sometime between 1582 and 1592 and performed by Lord Strange's Men for theatrical entrepreneur, Philip Henslowe in February 1592, it is one of the earlier Elizabethan revenge tragedies.

Overseeing the main action is the ghost of Don Andrea, who is seeking revenge for his death at the hands of Don Balthazar, Prince of Portingale*. He is accompanied by the personification of 'Revenge', who promises him vengeance and the opportunity to watch the tortuous route by which his enemy reaches his inevitable destruction.

Balthazar falls in love with the desirable Bel-Imperia, daughter of the Duke of Castile, but discovers she is already in love with Horatio, son of HIERONIMO, Knight Marshal of Spain. He conspires with Bel-Imperia's brother Lorenzo to kill Horatio.

In this scene HIERONIMO, having discovered his son's body and the identify of his murderers, is met by two Portingales who stop to ask him the way to Lorenzo's house. He answers them wildly in his speech**, which conveys the tension he is suffering under, but convinces the Portingales that he is 'passing lunatic'.

---

* Portugal

** This speech was added to the text in 1602 and expands Hieronimo's state of mind. Its authorship is uncertain.

Act 3, Scene 11

HIERONIMO

'Tis neither as you think, nor as you think,
Nor as you think: you're wide all:
These slippers are not mine, they were my son Horatio's.

My son, and what's a son? A thing begot
Within a pair of minutes, thereabout:
A lump bred up in darkness, and doth serve
To ballace these light creatures we call women;
And, at nine moneth's end, creeps forth to light.
What is there yet in a son
To make a father dote, rave or run mad?
Being born, it pouts, cries, and breeds teeth.
What is there yet in a son? He must be fed,
Be taught to go, and speak. Ay, or yet?
Why might not a man love a calf as well?
Or melt in passion o'er a frisking kid,
As for a son? Methinks a young bacon
Or a fine little smooth horse-colt
Should move a man as much as doth a son:
For one of these in very little time
Will grow to some good use, whereas a son,
The more he grows in stature and years,
The more unsquared, unbevelled he appears,
Reckons his parents among the rank of fools,
Strikes care upon their heads with his mad riots,
Makes them look old before they meet with age:
This is a son:
And what a loss were this, considered truly?
Oh, but my Horatio
Grew out of reach of these insatiate humours:
He loved his loving parents,
He was my comfort, and his mother's joy,
The very arm that did hold up our house:
Our hopes were stored up in him,
None but a damned murderer could hate him.

wide wide of the mark, quite wrong
ballace ballast, weigh down
moneths months (metre requires a dissyllable)
breeds teeth cuts teeth
go walk
Ay, or yet? Hieronimo means 'Yes, or what else?', 'What can I add?'
young bacon piglet
insatiate humours unsatisfied whims and caprices

113

'Tis Pity She's a Whore

John Ford

First published in 1633 and performed by The Queen's Company at the Phoenix in Drury Lane, London, sometime between 1629 and 1633. It is set in Parma and tells the story of the incestuous love between a brilliant young scholar, GIOVANNI, and his sister Annabella, ending in their tragic death and the destruction of those around them. In this opening scene, GIOVANNI confesses his feelings for Annabella to Friar Bonaventura, his friend and erstwhile tutor.

Act 1, Scene 1

GIOVANNI

                         ... Gentle father,
To you I have unclasped my burdened soul,
Emptied the storehouse of my thoughts and heart,
Made myself poor of secrets; have not left
Another word untold, which hath not spoke
All what I ever durst, or think, or know;
And yet is here the comfort I shall have,
Must I not do what all men else may, love?
                    ... Must I not praise
That beauty which, if framed anew, the gods
Would make a god of, if they had it there,
And kneel to it, as I do kneel to them?
                ... Shall a peevish sound,
A customary form, from man to man,
Of brother and of sister, be a bar
'Twixt my perpetual happiness and me?
Say that we had one father, say one womb
(Curse to my joys) gave both us life and birth;
Are we not therefore each to other bound
So much the more by nature? by the links
Of blood, of reason? nay, if you will have't,
Even of religion, to be ever one,
One soul, one flesh, one love, one heart, one all? ...
Shall then, for that I am her brother born,
My joys be ever banished from her bed?
No, father; in your eyes I see the change
Of pity and compassion; from your age,
As from a sacred oracle, distils
The life of counsel: tell me, holy man,
What cure shall give me ease in these extremes.

fond foolish
peevish trifling
customary form conventional formality

Volpone

Ben Jonson

First performed in 1605 by the King's Men and set in Venice. VOLPONE – the name means 'an old fox' – aided by his confederate, Mosca, sets out to dupe various legacy-hunters by pretending to be on his death-bed and promising to make each one of them his sole heir. To keep in his favour they bring rich offerings, each trying to outvie potential rivals. Throughout the action the flamboyant VOLPONE takes on more and more disguises and gets himself into preposterous situations in order to inveigle money and treasures from the gullible. In this opening scene he greets the morning and orders Mosca to 'open the shrine' so that he may worship his ill-gotten gains.

Act 1, Scene 1

VOLPONE
Good morning to the day; and, next, my gold!
Open the shrine, that I may see my saint.
[*Mosca reveals the treasure*]
Hail the world's soul, and mine! More glad than is
The teeming earth to see the longed-for sun
Peep through the horns of the celestial Ram,
Am I, to view thy splendour, darkening his;
That, lying here, amongst my other hoards,
Show'st like a flame, by night; or like the day
Struck out of Chaos, when all darkness fled
Unto the centre. O, thou sun of Sol,
But brighter than thy father, let me kiss,
With adoration, thee, and every relic
Of sacred treasure, in this blessed room.
Well did wise Poets, by thy glorious name
Title that age, which they would have the best;
Thou being the best of things; and far transcending
All style of joy in children, parents, friends,
Or any other waking dream on earth.
Thy looks when they to Venus did ascribe,
They should have given her twenty thousand Cupids;
Such are thy beauties, and our loves! Dear *saint*,
Riches, the dumb god, that giv'st all men tongues;
That canst do nought, and yet mak'st men do all things;
The price of souls; even hell, with thee to boot,
Is made worth heaven! Thou art virtue, fame,
Honour, and all things else! Who can get thee,
He shall be noble, valiant, honest, wise –

celestial Ram the sun enters Aries at the spring equinox
day . . . Chaos the first day of creation
sun of Sol alchemy held gold to be the offspring of the sun
relic i.e. the kind found in a shrine
that age the Golden Age
the dumb god 'silence is golden'

The Way of the World

William Congreve

This Restoration comedy was first presented at the Lincoln's Inn
Fields Theatre, London, in 1700 and is set in fashionable London.
The main action revolves around the courtship of the witty
and vivacious, Mrs Millamant by the more serious, but
'admirable' EDWARD MIRABELL. MIRABELL has had many
little 'intrigues' in the past, not least among them with the
unhappily married Mrs Fainall and the scheming Mrs Marwood,
but is now deeply in love with Millamant. He pursues her
throughout most of the play, while she teases and skilfully keeps
him at arm's length. In this scene he has cornered her at last.
She admits that she 'is on the verge of matrimony' but at the
same time insists on setting out her conditions of marriage. He
counters this with conditions of his own.

Act 4, Scene 1

MIRABELL
Your bill of fare is something advanced in this latter account. Well,
have I liberty to offer conditions, that when you are dwindled into
a wife, I may not be beyond measure enlarged into a husband? . . . I
thank you. *Imprimis* then, I covenant that your acquaintance be general; that you admit no sworn confidante or intimate of your own
sex, no she-friend to screen her affairs under your countenance and
tempt you to make trial of a mutual secrecy; no decoy-duck to whee-
dle you a fop, scrambling to the play in a mask, then bring you home
in a pretended fright when you think you shall be found out, and
rail at me for missing the play, and disappointing the frolic, which
you had to pick me up and prove my constancy! . . . *Item*, I article
that you continue to like your own face as long as I shall, and while
it passes current with me, that you endeavour not to new-coin it. To

118

which end, together with all vizards for the day, I prohibit all masks for the night made of oiled skins and I know not what – hog's bones, hare's gall, pig-water, and the marrow of a roasted cat. In short, I forbid all commerce with the gentlewoman in what-d'ye-call-it Court. *Item*, I shut my doors against all bawds with baskets, and pennyworth's of muslin, china, fans, atlases, etc. *Item*, when you shall be breeding – . . . I denounce against all strait-lacing, squeezing, for a shape, till you mould my boy's head like a sugar-loaf, and instead of a man-child make me the father to a crooked billet. Lastly, to the dominion of the tea table I submit, but with proviso that you exceed not in your province, but restrain yourself to native and simple tea table drinks, as tea, chocolate and coffee; as, likewise, to genuine and authorised tea table talk, such as mending of fashions, spoiling reputations, railing at absent friends, and so forth; but that on no account you encroach upon the men's prerogative and presume to drink healths or toast fellows; for prevention of which I banish all foreign forces, all auxiliaries to the tea table, as orange brandy, all aniseed, cinnamon, citron and Barbadoes waters, together with ratafia and the most noble spirit of clary. But, for cowslip wine, poppy water and all dormitives, those I allow. These provisos admitted, in other things I may prove a tractable and complying husband.

Imprimis in the first place; a term used in legal contracts.
atlases rich silk-satin from the Orient, flowered with gold or silver
strait-lacing tightly-laced corsets
sugar-loaf moulded hard refined sugar, in a conical mass; also applied figuratively to a conical hill and the conical Tudor and Stuart tall hat
billet small stick
orange brandy brandy flavoured with orange-peel
Barbadoes water brandy flavoured with orange and lemon peel
clary a drink made from brandy and clary flowers with the addition of sugar, cinnamon, and a little dissolved ambergris
dormitives drinks to induce sleep

The White Devil

John Webster

First performed early in 1612 by the Queen's Men at the Red Bull Theatre in Blackfriars, London, and set in Venice. FLAMINEO, ambitious and utterly ruthless, has procured his beautiful sister, Vittoria, for the Duke of Brachiano and, on the Duke's orders, murdered her husband and the Duchess. Now he has killed his younger brother, Marcello, after a quarrel, callously leaving his mother to remove the body. In the meantime, Brachiano, now married to Vittoria, is poisoned by his former wife's relatives.

At the beginning of this scene, Francisco, Duke of Florence, in his disguise as a Moor, leads FLAMINEO to where his mother, now mad with grief, is burying her son. As she and her ladies move away from the graveside, FLAMINEO admits to feeling compassion for her, but as soon as Francisco leaves him, begins to plan how to extract money from his now 'rich sister'. He is interrupted by the appearance of the ghost of Brachiano.

Act 5, Scene 4

FLAMINEO
I have a strange thing in me, to the which
I cannot give a name, without it be
Compassion; I pray leave me.
                              [*Exit Francisco*]
This night I'll know the utmost of my fate,
I'll be resolv'd what my rich sister means
T'assign me for my service. I have liv'd
Riotously ill, like some that live in court.
And sometimes, when my face was full of smiles
Have felt the maze of conscience in my breast.

120

Oft gay and honour'd robes these tortures try,
We think cag'd birds sing, when indeed they cry.
   [*Enter Brachiano's Ghost. In his leather cassock and breeches, boots,*
      a cowl (and in his hand) a pot of lily-flowers with a skull in't.]
Ha! I can stand thee. Nearer, nearer yet.
What mockery had death made of thee? Thou look'st sad.
In what place art thou? in yon starry gallery,
Or in the cursed dungeon? No? not speak?
Pray, sir, resolve me, what religion's best
For a man to die in? or is it in your knowledge
To answer me how long I have to live?
That's the most necessary question.
Not answer? Are you still like some great men
That only walk like shadows up and down,
And to no purpose: say: –
[*The ghost throws earth upon him and shows him the skull*]
What's that? O fatal! He throws earth upon me.
A dead man's skull beneath the roots of flowers.
I pray speak sir; our Italian churchmen
Make us believe, dead men hold conference
With their familiars, and many times
Will come to bed to them, and eat with them. [*Exit ghost*]
He's gone; and see, the skull and earth are vanish'd.
This is beyond melancholy. I do dare my fate
To do its worst. Now to my sister's lodging,
And sum up all these horrors; the disgrace
The Prince threw on me; next the piteous sight
Of my dead brother; and my mother's dotage;
And last this terrible vision. All these
Shall with Vittoria's bounty turn to good,
Or I will drown this weapon in her blood.

familiars familiar spirits; close friends or relations

121

The Witch

Thomas Middleton

This Jacobean tragi-comedy was probably written in 1615 or 1616 and performed by the King's Men at Blackfriars, London. It is set in Ravenna, a token location which could as easily be London, with its satire of life at Court and the King's obsession with witchcraft. The Witch, Hecate and her sisters are highly comic characters who are visited frequently by the nobility in their quest for charms, love potions and poisons. SEBASTIAN has just returned from three years at war to find that his beloved Isabella, who was contracted to be his wife, is being married that very day to Antonio.

In this scene he approaches Hecate and begs her to prevent the marriage being consummated that night.

Act 1, Scene 2

SEBASTIAN

[*Aside*] Heaven knows with what unwillingness and hate
I enter this damned place – but such extremes
Of wrongs in love fight 'gainst religious knowledge,
That were I led by this disease to deaths
As numberless as creatures that must die,
I could not shun the way. I know what 'tis
To pity madmen now. They're wretched things
That ever were created, if they be
Of woman's making and her faithless vows.
I fear they're now a-kissing. What's o'clock?
'Tis now but supper-time, but night will come –
And all new-married couples make short suppers.
[*To Hecate*] Whate'er thou art, I have no spare time to fear thee;
My horrors are so strong and great already,
That thou seem'st nothing. Up and laze not.
Hadst thou my business, thou couldst ne'er sit so;
'Twould firk thee into air a thousand mile
Beyond thy ointments. I would I were read
So much in thy black power as mine own griefs.
I'm in great need of help; wilt give me any?

firk jerk, beat, whip
ointments for flying

The Witch

Thomas Middleton

This Jacobean tragi-comedy was probably written in 1615 or 1616
and performed by The King's Men at Blackfriars, London. It is
set in Ravenna, a token location which could easily be London,
with its satire of life at Court and the King's obsession with
witchcraft. The Witch, Hecate and her sisters are highly comic
characters who are patronised regularly by the nobility.
ALMACHILDES, described as a fantastical gentleman, foppish
in his attire, is very drunk when he visits Hecate to obtain a
love charm to seduce Amoretta, the Duchess' woman. Hecate,
lusting after ALMACHILDES, persuades him to stay to supper.
In this scene he is recovering from his night with the witches
and finds the love charm in his pocket.

Act 2, Scene 2

ALMACHILDES
What a mad toy took me to sup with witches?
Fie of all drunken humours! By this hand,
I could beat myself when I think on't – and the rascals
Made me good cheer too, and to my understanding then
Ate some of every dish and spoiled the rest.
But coming to my lodging I remember
I was as hungry as a tired foot-post.
                         [*Takes a ribbon from his pocket*]
What's this? Oh 'tis the charm her hagship gave me
For my duchess' obstinate woman, wound about
A threepenny silk ribbon of three colours:
[*Reads*] *Necte tribus nodis ternos, Amoretta, colores.*
Amoretta – why there's her name indeed –
Necte, Amoretta – again, two bouts –

Nodo et 'Veneris' dic 'vincula necte' –
Nay, if *Veneris* be one, I'm sure there's no dead flesh in't.
If I should undertake to construe this now,
I should make a fine piece of work of it;
For few young gallants are given to good construction
Of anything – hardly of their best friends' wives,
Sisters or nieces. Let me see what I can do now.
Necte tribus nodis – Nick of the tribe of noddies –
Ternos colores – that makes turned colours –
Nodo et Veneris – goes to his venery like a noddy –
Dic Vincula – with Dick the vintner's boy.

Here were a sweet charm now if this were the meaning on't, and
very likely to overcome an honourable gentlewoman. The whoreson
old hellcat would have given me the brain of a cat once in my hand-
kercher I bad her make sauce with't, with a vengeance! – and a little bone in the nethermost part of a wolf's tail – I bad her pick her
teeth with't, with a pestilence! Nay, this is somewhat cleanly yet and
handsome; a coloured ribbon – a fine, gentle charm – a man may
give't his sister, his brother's wife, ordinarily.

[*Enter Amoretta*]

See, here she comes, luckily.

---

toy foolish, fantastic notion
to . . . then from what I (in my drunken state) could make sense of
spoiled messed up
foot-post foot courier
bouts knots or twists
dead flesh bawdy, i.e. the flesh will rise to the occasion
construe explain, translate
noddies fools, simpletons
vintner wine-merchant
cleanly neat

A Woman Killed with Kindness

Thomas Heywood

First performed in 1604 and set in Yorkshire, it is the story of a 'perfect wife's' infidelity with her husband's 'trusted friend', and the unusual punishment meted out to her by her husband's extreme kindness, which eventually leads to her death.

In this scene, JOHN FRANKFORD, a good husband and much respected gentleman, has been informed by his servant, Nicholas, that his wife is being unfaithful to him with his friend, Wendoll. At first he is angry and sends Nicholas away. Once alone, doubts set in, but he determines to dismiss these from his thoughts until he has obtained further proof.

Scene 8

FRANKFORD
Thy eyes may be deceived I tell thee,
For should an angel from the heavens drop down
And preach this to me that thyself hast told,
He should have much ado to win belief,
In both their loves I am so confident . . .
No more; to supper, and command your fellows
To attend us and the strangers. Not a word,
I charge thee on thy life; be secret then,
For I know nothing . . .

                                          [*Exit Nick*]

Away, be gone.
She is well born, descended nobly,
Virtuous her education, her repute
Is in the general voice of all the country
Honest and fair, her carriage, her demeanour
In all her actions that concern the love
To me, her husband, modest, chaste, and godly.
Is all this seeming gold plain copper?
But he, that Judas that hath borne my purse,
And sold me for a sin – O God, O God,
Shall I put up these wrongs? No, shall I trust
The bare report of this suspicious groom
Before the double gilt, the well hatch ore
Of their two hearts? No, I will loose these thoughts.
Distraction I will banish from my brow,
And from my looks exile sad discontent.
Their wonted favours in my tongue shall flow.
Till I know all, I'll nothing seem to know.
Lights and a table there! Wife, Master Wendoll and
gentle Master Cranwell –

strangers guests, visitors
put up submit to, endure, suffer quietly
groom serving-man

A Woman of No Importance

Oscar Wilde

This society comedy or comedy of manners was first produced in 1893 at the Haymarket Theatre, London, and is set mainly at Hunstanton Chase, the English country home of the influential Lady Hunstanton. GERALD ARBUTHNOT, a young bank clerk, has been offered the position of secretary to Lord Illingworth. His mother is enthusiastic about this unexpected opportunity for her son until she meets Lord Illingworth and recognises him as George Barford, her lover of twenty years ago who refused to marry her and is also Gerald's natural father. In this scene she begs GERALD to turn down the appointment, saying that she can't bear to be left on her own. GERALD, unable to understand this sudden change in his mother, accuses her of trying to crush his ambition.

Act 3

GERALD

Don't put it like that, mother. Of course I am sorry to leave you. Why, you are the best mother in the whole world. But after all, as Lord Illingworth says, it is impossible to live in such a place as Wrockley. You don't mind it. But I'm ambitious; I want something more than that. I want to have a career. I want to do something that will make you proud of me, and Lord Illingworth is going to help me. He is going to do everything for me ... Mother, how changeable you are! You don't seem to know your own mind for a single moment. An hour and a half ago in the drawing-room you agreed to the whole thing; now you turn round and make objections, and try to force me to give up my one chance in life. Yes, my one chance. You don't suppose that men like Lord Illingworth are to be found every day, do you, mother? It is very strange that when I have had such a wonderful piece of good luck, the one person to put difficulties in my way should be my own mother. Besides, you know, mother, I love Hester Worsley. Who could help loving her? I love her more than I ever told you, far more. And if I had a position, if I had prospects, I could – I could ask her to – Don't you understand now, mother, what it means to me to be Lord Illingworth's secretary? To start like that is to find a career ready for one – before one – waiting for one. If I were Lord Illingworth's secretary I could ask Hester to be my wife. As a wretched bank clerk with a hundred a year it would be an impertinence ... You have always tried to crush my ambition, mother – haven't you? You have told me that the world is a wicked place, that success is not worth having, that society is shallow, and all that sort of thing – well, I don't believe it, mother. I think the world must be delightful. I think society must be exquisite. I think success is a thing worth having. You have been wrong in all that you taught me, mother, quite wrong. Lord Illingworth is a successful man. He is a fashionable man. He is a man who lives in the world and for it. Well, I would give anything to be just like Lord Illingworth.

Women Beware Women

Thomas Middleton

There is no record of this Jacobean revenge tragedy until well after Middleton's death, but it was most probably written in 1621 and performed with great success. A play of love, lust, incest and revenge, it exposes the position of women in a world where, at best, they are simply the property of men whatever their social status may be. LEANTIO, a not very successful commercial agent, has eloped with Bianca, a young and beautiful Venetian heiress, and taken her back home to live with him and his elderly mother. She is seen by the Duke of Florence, who falls in love with her, seduces her and makes her his mistress.

In this banquet scene, LEANTIO realises that he has lost Bianca for ever. She is now officially the Duke's mistress and he has been offered the Captaincy of the fort at Rouans by way of compensation. The guests leave and LEANTIO is alone with Livia, an older but still desirable woman, who is determined to seduce him. He speaks his thoughts aloud, hardly aware of her presence.

Act 3, Scene 2

LEANTIO

[*Aside*] Oh hast thou left me then, Bianca, utterly!
Bianca! Now I miss thee. Oh return,
And save the faith of woman! I nev'r felt
The loss of thee till now; 'tis an affliction
Of greater weight than youth was made to bear,
As if a punishment of after-life
Were fall'n upon man here; so new it is
To flesh and blood, so strange, so insupportable
A torment, ev'n mistook, as if a body
Whose death were drowning must needs therefore suffer it
In scalding oil.
                        . . . As long as mine eye saw thee,
I half enjoyed thee.
                        . . . Canst thou forget
The dear pains my love took, how it has watched
Whole nights together in all weathers for thee,
Yet stood in heart more merry than the tempests
That sung about mine ears, like dangerous flatterers
That can set all their mischief to sweet tunes;
And then received thee from thy father's window
Into these arms at midnight, when we embraced
As if we had been statues only made for't,
To show art's life, so silent were our comforts,
And kissed as if our lips had grown together! . . .
[*Aside*] Canst thou forget all this? And better joys
That we met after this, which then new kisses
Took pride to praise? . . .
This cannot be but of some close bawd's working.
[*To Livia*] Cry mercy, lady. What would you say to me?
My sorrow makes me so unmannerly,
So comfort bless me, I had quite forgot you.

A torment, ev'n mistook mistaken torment
only made for't only made for embracing
show art's life to show how lifelike the artwork is
close secret

Index of playwrights

Anon
  Arden of Faversham
  The Revenger's Tragedy
Francis Beaumont
  The Knight of the Burning Pestle
Aphra Behn
  The Rover
George Chapman
  Bussy D'Ambois
William Congreve
  The Double-Dealer
  Love for Love
  The Way of the World
Thomas Dekker
  The Shoemaker's Holiday
John Dryden
  All for Love
George Farquhar
  The Beaux' Stratagem
John Ford
  The Broken Heart
  'Tis Pity She's a Whore
Oliver Goldsmith
  She Stoops to Conquer
Thomas Heywood
  A Woman Killed with Kindness
Ben Jonson
  The Alchemist
  Bartholmew Fair
  Epicoene *or* The Silent Woman
  Volpone
Ben Jonson, George Chapman &
John Marston
  Eastward Ho!
Thomas Kyd
  The Spanish Tragedy

Christopher Marlowe
  Dr Faustus
  Edward the Second
John Marston
  The Malcontent
Philip Massinger
  A New Way to Pay Old Debts
Thomas Middleton
  The Witch
  Women Beware Women
Thomas Middleton & William
Rowley
  The Changeling
Mr S.
  Gammer Gurton's Needle
Richard Brinsley Sheridan
  The Critic
  The Rivals
  The School for Scandal
Cyril Tourneur
  The Atheist's Tragedy
John Vanbrugh
  The Provoked Wife
  The Relapse
John Webster
  The Duchess of Malfi
  The White Devil
Oscar Wilde
  An Ideal Husband
  The Importance of Being Earnest
  Lady Windermere's Fan
  A Woman of No Importance
William Wycherley
  The Country Wife
  The Plain Dealer

ORDER FORM

The New Mermaid play texts can be ordered from your local book-seller or direct from our warehouse. In the USA and Canada customers can order the play texts through W.W. Norton & Company, 500 Fifth Avenue, New York NY 10110.

The Alchemist Ben Jonson £4.99
All for Love John Dryden £4.99
Arden of Faversham Anon £4.99
The Atheist's Tragedy Cyril Tourneur £4.99
Bartholmew Fair Ben Jonson £5.99
The Beaux' Stratagem George Farquhar £4.99
The Broken Heart John Ford £5.99
Bussy D'Ambois George Chapman £4.99
The Changeling Thomas Middleton & William Rowley £4.99
The Country Wife William Wycherley £4.99
The Critic Richard Brinsley Sheridan £4.99
The Double-Dealer William Congreve £4.99
Dr Faustus Christopher Marlowe £4.99
The Duchess of Malfi John Webster £4.99
Eastward Ho! Ben Jonson, George Chapman & John Marston £5.99
Edward the Second Christopher Marlowe £4.99
Epicoene or *The Silent Woman* Ben Jonson £5.99
Gammer Gurton's Needle Mr S. £5.99
An Ideal Husband Oscar Wilde £5.99
The Importance of Being Earnest Oscar Wilde £4.99
The Knight of the Burning Pestle Francis Beaumont £4.99
Lady Windermere's Fan Oscar Wilde £4.99
Love for Love William Congreve £4.99
The Malcontent John Marston £4.99
A New Way to Pay Old Debts Philip Massinger £5.99
The Plain Dealer William Wycherley £4.99
The Provoked Wife John Vanbrugh £5.99
The Relapse John Vanbrugh £5.99
The Revenger's Tragedy Anon £4.99
The Rivals Richard Brinsley Sheridan £4.99
The Rover Aphra Behn £5.99

The School for Scandal Richard Brinsley Sheridan £4.99
She Stoops to Conquer Oliver Goldsmith £4.99
The Shoemaker's Holiday Thomas Dekker £4.99
The Spanish Tragedy Thomas Kyd £4.99
'Tis Pity She's a Whore John Ford £4.99
Volpone Ben Jonson £4.99
The Way of the World William Congreve £4.99
The White Devil John Webster £5.99
The Witch Thomas Middleton £5.99
A Woman Killed with Kindness Thomas Heywood £4.99
A Woman of No Importance Oscar Wilde £5.99
Women Beware Women Thomas Middleton £5.99

Tick the title(s) you want and fill in the form below.
Prices and availability subject to change without notice

Please return to **A & C Black (Publishers) Limited, PO Box 19, Huntingdon, Cambs PE19 3SF tel (01480) 212666 fax (01480) 405014**

Send a cheque or postal order for the value of the book(s), adding (for postage and packing at the printed paper rate) 15% UK and Eire; 20% overseas.
Airmail rates available on application

Or please debit this amount from my Access/Visa Card (delete as appropriate)

Card number

Amount _____ Expiry date

Signed _____

Name (please print)_____

Address_____

_____ Postcode _____